Managing the Primary Classroom

Editor: Ian Craig

Contributors

Ray Arnold, John Barrett, John Bird, Sybil Coward, Ian Craig,
Helen Gillespie, Kath Rollisson, Iain Smithers, Eric Spear,
Heather Toynbee, Tony Wainwright, Clive Wilkinson.

Longman

In association with
The National Association of Head Teachers

Longman Group UK Limited
Longman House, Burnt Mill, Harlow, Essex, CM20 2JE

First published 1987

British Library Cataloguing in Publication Data

Craig, Ian
  Managing the primary classroom.
  1. Classroom management——Great Britain
  2. Teachers——Great Britain 3. Elementary
  schools——Great Britain
  I. Title
  372.16′21   LB3013

ISBN 0-582-02233-9

Printed and bound in Great Britain by Page Bros (Norwich) Ltd

CONTENTS

Acknowledgements

We are grateful to the following for permission to reproduce copyright material:

Addison-Wesley Publishing Co. Inc. for fig 1.1 from p 22 *Managing The Marginal and Unsatisfactory Performer* by L. L. Steinmetz (2nd ed., 1985) © Addison-Wesley Publishing Co. Inc., 1985; Kent County Council Education Committee for record sheets from the *Kent Maths Project* © Kent County Council 1979; Nuffield-Chelsea Curriculum Trust for a Stage 2 Record Sheet from *Nuffield Maths 5–11* (pub Longman Group Ltd, 1983).

Re-defining the basics

Two recent publications from the DES, the spirit of which, it seems to me, is in direct conflict with the 'reforms' of the current Secretary of State's national curriculum (with testing at ages 7, 11, 14 and 16 years) describe good practice in a wide range of schools observed by HMI. In *Primary Schools – Some Aspects of Good Practice* (1987) teachers are commended for the extent to which they emphasise the importance of thinking and encourage children 'to reflect upon and organise their thinking about the activities and experiences which are provided for them'. In another DES booklet, entitled *Education Observed 3 – Good Teachers* (1985), HMI comment:

> Teaching well matched to pupils' abilities and needs will produce desirable results in terms much wider than examination grades and achievements which are matched to the pupils' abilities across a wide range of performance while reflecting challenge and rigour at all levels. It is by these wide measures of pupil performance including attitudes and personal and social responsibility that teachers' success should be judged.

Judging from the many examples of good practice observed by HMI, it would appear that there was recognition that, in the complex task facing them, many teachers were doing not too bad a job; that where there was an investigation of the 'informality' and 'freedoms' associated with good practice, these were not there merely by chance but were the means whereby 'self-discipline was being nurtured'; that where the teaching style was 'over-didactic and rigid' it produced 'boredom' in the pupils because they were rarely expected to be actively involved in what was going on; that quantifiable test scores in evaluating the educational progress of young children were too limiting and that self-assessment should be encouraged.

Better Schools (1985), also produced by the DES, declares a concern that in a majority of primary schools, 'there is over-concentration on practising basic skills in literacy and numeracy without relating them to real situations'. Is it at all conceivable that the national curriculum and its testing arrangements from the age of seven will do anything to alleviate this worrying state of affairs?

So what are the 'basics' for children in their early encounters with institutionalised education? To my mind the focus of all our work with children in the primary years should be the promotion of effective thinking and feeling, because without these there cannot be effective learning. Brearley (1972) presents a useful analysis of some attributes of a good thinker. In planning and evaluating the effectiveness of teaching it is helpful to consider characteristics of good thinking and how best to promote these in the classroom. A

Introduction

In recent years the Department of Education and Science has targetted 'Management' as a key area for the in-service training of teachers. At present, most initiatives in this area are directed towards headteachers and senior staff in schools, and towards the management of the school as a whole.

It is the view of many people in the education service that to improve the management of the whole school one ought to begin by improving the management of individual classrooms.

In response to this, local authorities are now beginning to organise 'management' courses for classroom teachers. Teachers themselves are also beginning to realise that a knowledge of the principles of 'management', and its implications, is important for their own professional development.

Some practitioners will undoubtedly misunderstand calls on them to improve their management skills, unsure of how this learning will make them become better teachers. Whatever their preconceptions, they will all agree that it is their role to provide the most stimulating environment possible for the children in their charge. Management is the organisation of that environment, and teachers need to take it seriously if they are seeking to improve the quality of teaching and learning.

This book tries to identify key areas in the organisation of classrooms, and to suggest developments that might take place to improve that organisation. Each chapter has been written from experience, by a practitioner in the field of primary education. All the contributors are, or have been headteachers of primary schools. Those who are not now headteachers go into a variety of schools during the course of their work, and are still well informed on the realities of life 'at the chalk face'. In this book there should be no 'credibility gap' often found between the writers and readers of books for primary teachers.

By using a team of writers with wide and diverse experience, it has been possible to explore important topics in some depth. Inevitably, some of the writers cover similar ground, and sometimes expound conflicting ideas. In this book, such conflict has not been consciously avoided. It is however interesting to note just how closely the different contributors agree on many aspects.

It is usual for books on teaching to be sequential – it is necessary to read earlier parts of the book to understand later parts. Chapters in this book are self-contained, and can be read in any order. No chapter is too long not to be read in one sitting, and most end with a booklist for the interested reader to follow up particularly interesting ideas.

This book is intended to inform *and* to change practice. Many of the chapters give practical ideas for readers to use in their own classrooms. It is not intended to be an 'academic' work, to be used only by teachers following courses in education, but a book to be read by *all* those involved in teaching in primary schools as part of their normal professional reading. It is hoped that it is of equal value to the experienced teacher and to the teacher following a course of initial training.

Throughout the book, for consistency of style, all teachers (including headteachers) have been referred to as *she*, and all pupils as *he*.

Ian Craig

1 Organising for effective learning

Kath Rollisson

There is no doubt that teaching is becoming an increasingly com task. It is therefore the intention to attempt to cover in this cha some issues about children learning and about the ordi everyday problems of classroom management teachers fa planning, organising and implementing an effective lea environment. Since the mid 1970s and the Ruskin speech, tea have been bombarded with a plethora of advice and sugge from all sides: 'back to basics', 'too much playing about in sc these days', 'no more of this open-plan nonsense', 'what ch need is four walls and a classroom door that can be shut', 'no w reading standards are dropping', etc.

There is, however, no evidence in research or theory to s the argument that a narrowing down of the curriculum will a higher standards of attainment in young children. In fac reports of school inspections, for instance, indicate tha concentration on the teaching of basic skills to the exclusion c areas of the curriculum does not produce the best results. C need opportunities to apply skills if they are to lear thoroughly. In order to apply skills effectively, children r environment in which learning is irresistible; one which will the necessary motivation; one in which the process of learn exciting that they recognise the need to acquire certain skills to participate fully in what is on offer. It is the relevance of th that is crucial. Smith (1971) talking about children learning says 'Children will not stop learning anything that is mear them, unless the learning becomes too difficult or too c them, in which case the learning itself becomes meaningle good thinker is usually confident, so there is value in the teacher using all possible means to foster a confident attitude in children. When a child approaches a problem with confidence in his own ability to solve it, he brings to the task a special sort of energy which is likely to be productive. If this confidence is rooted in previous success, it will encourage persistence even after several attempts because earlier experiences indicate that effort brings a solution. The teacher may need to arrange for success to be made explicit, but where a confident attitude is positively encouraged a child is ready to see mistakes and failures as essential stages in the learning process. Proponents of age-related testing who seek, through a national system of testing, to encourage comparisons and so brand about half our children 'below average', i.e., failures at as early as 7 years, haplessly ignoring the fact that they develop physically, emotionally and intellectually at different rates, will have much to answer for. They cannot have considered the wider social implications.

Another characteristic of a good thinker is independence. Children can be encouraged to operate independently from a very early age. We sometimes greatly underestimate their considerable abilities to take responsibility for their own actions and so 'spoonfeed' them. Independent attitudes and ways of working are not achieved without much support and guidance. It is not just a question of 'letting them get on with it'. Independence depends on good classroom organisation. If children become accustomed to having materials handed to them and if they are always told everything they need to know and are not encouraged to find out for themselves, it will be difficult for them to develop independence.

Concentration is another attribute of a good thinker. From the earliest stages there is value in any task which evokes concentration in the child because the habit, once acquired, can be transferred to other learning situations. How can the teacher foster the power to become absorbed in a task? One way is to take note of the materials and activities which extend the span of concentration and then provide fully for these. By timely introduction of a new piece of apparatus, such as a curved block in constructional activities or a hand lens in the science area, to enable better examination of a spider's movement, or by a sensitive comment or question, the teacher can prolong the time spent on a task and so deepen and extend the level of a child's concentration.

Children need a framework of support for their learning and thinking within which they can exercise and extend their responsibility for themselves. They need a knowledge of what is permitted and of the reasons behind any rules operating as constraints. They have a keen sense of justice. They need to develop a feeling of their own personal worth with respect for self and others.

It is imperative that schools provide a child with a meaning for living and a framework which will help him to choose and act with wisdom.

A further characteristic of good thinking is the ability to estimate, to analyse, to synthesise, to make judgements, and to make and test hypotheses about all manner of concepts and forms of understanding with all the crucial related language development. Brearley (1972) says that schools should be seeking to develop an 'organic' growth of language in children, one which is rooted in personal, first-hand experiences which 'provoke the need for new words for their definition'. It is accepted that children must learn to read, write and spell, but communication at a much deeper level is necessary if language is to be seen as a means of gaining new knowledge and developing thinking.

Some characteristics of good practice

There have been many attempts to define the characteristics of a good school. HMI, researchers and others involved in evaluating the work of primary schools have attempted to describe these. In a good school, teachers work together with a clear sense of direction and unity of purpose. There is strong leadership from the head. There is an absence of compartmentalism both in thinking and in approaches to the curriculum. Within this framework there is tolerance and respect for the views of others with the encouragement of individual enterprise, initiative and autonomy. A good school has clear aims about what children need to learn and about what constitutes purposeful, productive teaching. There are clear guidelines which are implemented and evaluated in terms of their effect on the teaching and learning taking place, and there is a close match between documents and practice. Teachers have time for discussion and to support each others' weaknesses as well as to foster and use any strengths. In good schools teachers are not servants to fashionable ideas about how children ought to learn. They seek to extend their knowledge by attendance at in-service courses but carefully evaluate the extent to which ideas and suggestions may, or may not, inform their practice. They are flexible and eclectic in their approach, using a wide variety of methods to stimulate children to act and think in a purposeful, rigorous way. Good teachers are 'clued up'. They have a sound knowledge of the educational process, of how children learn. They have a professional concern and respect for what each individual child has to offer and provide an atmosphere in which it is safe to fail and in which each child is helped to overcome his limitations. They understand that indiscipline occurs when children are bored and that tasks presented need to be matched at the appropriate level of ability and interest if they are to motivate children. These are just some elements of practice in good schools and indicate clearly the complex role of the primary teacher.

Aspects of organisation for effective teaching

The School Curriculum in Humberside (1986) describes the environment for learning which should exist in schools:

> From the early years of education it is essential that the skills and concepts are acquired in the context of a stimulating environment for learning which makes optimum use of first hand experience. These conditions will facilitate the development of imagination and creativity, and will also ensure that each child develops positive attitudes towards the learning process.

How can teachers best organise for this effective learning environment? It is crucial that the organisation which operates fits the school. Real difficulties can arise when a pattern which is ideally suited to one system is superimposed upon another for which it is totally inappropriate. Taylor (1983) identifies two important considerations about organisation, 'The individual teacher's own skill and quality outweigh all else in determining the success of the organisation, and there is no blueprint for successful organisation, no single foolproof system guaranteed to work in all circumstances with every teacher and every child in every school.' There are, however, some common elements that are identifiable as well as difficulties that can be overcome by a systematic approach.

Organisation should be the servant, not the master; supporting the purposes of teaching and learning, not dictating them. It should help children learn better. If it does not do this it fails. It is important to evaluate how well the organisation fits the school, not the reverse. In some schools an organisational pattern has taken over and has become more important than the things the teacher is trying to achieve. Organisation must arise from a clearly defined philosophy. There is no special merit in itself in an integrated day, for example. An integrated day, if applied rigidly and without thought to the quality of the experiences provided or the match of task to the abilities and interests of the children, can be as inappropriate to the learning needs of the individual as the most inflexible of formal methods. Organisation must enable the teacher to meet a wide range of needs from the most able to the least able. In a falling rolls situation, teachers are often having to cope with a much wider age and ability range than previously. Class teaching aimed at a so-called norm would be inappropriate for the majority of the time, though it might be suitable on occasion. Group teaching is sometimes an effective way of meeting these needs as is an integrated or differentiated approach.

Another vital aspect of organisation is that it must be time effective. A portion of time is saved if children know where materials are kept, and if they are readily accessible and clearly labelled. In order to meet that wide range of needs, the teacher needs to be released from routine tasks, like giving out pencils and books, which children are well able to carry out themselves. Good organisation can provide more time. Routines which are familiar and accepted by the children should be established, so that a situation in which they are constantly asking what to do next can be avoided. A queue at the teacher's desk is a clear indication of bad organisation.

If there is a range of supplementary activities for the children to move on to, if they know where to go for the things they need to continue, if they have real responsibility delegated to them and are encouraged to be self-pacing and to use initiative, they will become self-reliant and develop increasing skill as independent agents of their own learning. Teachers need to evaluate carefully how time is spent by children in the classroom. Organisation must create opportunities for actual teaching of groups. Teachers often go from one extreme to the other in their teaching; in attempting to move away from a whole-class approach they try to teach entirely individually. In this situation they merely develop coping strategies and become totally ineffective in their teaching. Organisation is about grouping and re-grouping. The teacher must ensure that while she is working with one group, children in other groups are involved in tasks that are purposeful and developmental and are taking them forward in their thinking. What is necessary is for a range of activities from those that are teacher dependent to those that are not, i.e. groups working at varying levels of dependence on the teacher. Here careful planning is crucial.

Organisation needs

- well organised and structured resources;
- a system which children know how to operate;
- a range of supplementary activities;
- effective use of classroom space;
- an established routine that tasks begun are completed, though not necessarily to a time limit.

Some suggestions for organising an effective learning environment

In any system of organisation, it helps to identify areas of the classroom which are designated for different activities and experiences, and in which appropriate materials are readily available for the children to use. The model described below can be viewed as an introductory one in the move towards more integrated forms of classroom organisation. The division of the room into three areas is not intended to be restrictive. It is recognised that topic, CDT, environmental work, music and drama will be slotted in to whichever area is deemed appropriate at any one time, according to the children's learning needs.

Language area

Here will be situated a wide range of facilities for reading, writing and the development of oral language (recognising that these will be taking place in all areas). In this area will be a good supply of books – picture, story, poetry, fiction and reference. There will be attractive displays including collections of varied materials, e.g. glass, wood, fossils, sculptures, musical instruments, paintings and other art forms, maybe also insects and animals. Plenty of vocabulary arising out of first-hand or other experiences the children may have had, can be displayed – examples are captions, labels, interest sheets or booklets and word banks filed alphabetically or according to a theme. Interesting additions to stimulate imaginative ideas for oral or written expression may include a magic cave, a time machine, a space capsule, an airport, a shipwreck, etc. All the reading material and any structured language materials can be sited in this area, including tape recorders and word processors as well as paper and books of different shapes and sizes for writing of all kinds. Smith (1971) has produced a fascinating list of materials to ensure that children beginning to read are immersed in meaningful written language. These may be collected by teachers and children together and include:

stories to be enjoyed publicly and privately
books to be typed and bound
poems to be recited
songs to be sung
plays to be acted
encyclopaedias to be browsed in
notes to be passed
letters to be delivered
cartons to be labelled
lists to be constructed
sports scores to be recorded
events to be reported
newspapers to be circulated
instructions to be followed
enterprises to be planned

messages to be exchanged
bills to be collected
posters to be displayed
entertainment guides to be consulted
diaries to be concealed.

Mathematics/science area

Environmental provision in this area can help to ensure that children develop a positive attitude to mathematics as an interesting and enjoyable subject, and that they develop the skill of clear, logical thinking in mathematics, with confidence, independence and creativity. In the early years and beyond, a wide range of materials and equipment, which should be accessible and clearly labelled, is essential. Objects for counting, measuring and weighing; balances and other measures for volume and capacity work including standard and non-standard units should be available. Materials should include shells, stones and pebbles of various sizes and shapes, buttons of all kinds, conkers, cotton reels, counters, shells, cones, stop clocks, tocker timers, ribbons, plastic strips, containers of all kinds, calculators, suitable structural apparatus and selected computer software.

A science area with materials for CDT can also be combined with the mathematics area. Items of equipment might include magnets, bulbs, batteries, cogs, wheels, old car parts, clocks, televisions and almost any form of clockwork, mechanical, electrical and safe chemical objects which may fuel children's imagination and curiosity. Microscopes, magnifiers and viewers of all types are useful. Frogs, insects, fish and animals may also be included but it is important that children are encouraged to develop a sense of responsibility and sensitivity in the care of such creatures. Relevant reference books, books and fact sheets made by the children to provide information and computer data bases are useful.

Creative area

This will be a practical area in which all creative art activities take place, which, with an integrated approach, will be linked with topic and other work in various parts of the classroom. A sink with running water will be essential. Materials for painting, collage, clay, structural and three-dimensional models, pens, pencils, charcoal, fabrics and threads of all kinds for weaving, etc. will be located here as well as various tools and adhesives. All will be clearly labelled and stored so that they are easily accessible to children and can be replaced by them after use. There will be easels, places for finished work to be stored and supplies of paper and card of different sizes, shapes and qualities. A collection of objects and artefacts (items of aesthetic appeal as well as others which are functional and may be sited in other parts of the classroom) can be used to stimulate direct observational work.

Adjacent to this area if appropriate, particularly in an infant school, there could be located a place for cooking and an area for developmental play activities which may 'become' a dentist's surgery, bicycle repair shop or hairdressing salon as well as a traditional home corner. Natural and manufactured materials in addition to sand and water can be used by children of all ages for constructional, investigatory and problem-solving activities related to particular lines of enquiry or topic work.

It is important that thought and care be given to the quality of environmental provision in each area. Despite the specific designation of curriculum areas, there will be considerable overlap if learning is not to become fragmented and compartmentalised. In operating such a system, as a first stage in moving away from traditional class-based work towards a differentiated or integrated approach, it may be appropriate to divide the children into three groups and the day into three large blocks of time, two in the morning and one in the afternoon. This may be flexible, however. For instance, the teacher may wish to create a larger number of groups and areas with periods of time varying over one day or several days. Later it may be appropriate to develop a system whereby each child works to a negotiated personal timetable with tasks completed over an extended period.

Groups will be organised so that each moves to each curriculum area in turn during the course of a day. For the successful implementation of this approach, the groups will need to be operating at varying levels of dependence on the teacher. It will not be possible for the teacher to give total undivided attention to every child in every group at any one time. For this reason it is essential that planning and preparation are meticulous. Clear explanations and demonstrations of how the system works should be given to children. Do they really know what they are expected to do? Teachers sometimes fail to talk through such things and underrate children's considerable reasoning and logical abilities. Much support and encouragement, however, will be essential if they are to become self-pacing. If the teacher has carefully thought through the activities and experiences provided for the children, much relevant, meaningful learning can take place with every child purposefully occupied in tasks well suited to his level of interest and ability.

In this way one of the groups will be working independently with only occasional intervention from the teacher. A second group will be organised to work so that the children function largely unsupervised for some of the time but may need intermittent help during the allotted period. A third group will be involved with the teacher for the majority of the allotted time and will be closely supervised. This will ensure that each child, regularly and systematically, has a period when the teacher attends to personal progress on a one-to-one basis. A range of supplementary activities must be available for all children with a balance between free choice and direction. It may be that the teacher decides that the language group will receive the closest attention on one particular day. On another day this level of attention will be given to a different curriculum area, whichever is the priority at the time. It might be appropriate to draw the children together intermittently as a full class group to discuss work being undertaken, or to watch a well-presented demonstration by teacher or children. Any points about organisation, use of equipment and audio-visual materials can be clarified at such times. This might take place at the beginning of the day or period but that is not always necessary if there is continuity of learning from the previous session. Children often enjoy returning to a familiar task or piece of work at the start of the day. Class group times are also useful for the launch of a particular line of enquiry, a key lesson or introduction to a theme. An interest or news sheet or notes on forward planning to which teacher and children contribute can be compiled. If learning is to be truly child centred, children should be fully involved in negotiating and evaluating their own learning. The period after afternoon break is used in many schools for story, poetry, drama and music, which can be integrated. That is also a convenient time to review the day's activities and plan for the next stage. In the development towards more flexible approaches with personal timetables and periods extended over several days, this time can be used for a group session. The use of the hall or resources area for music, dance, drama and PE can be timetabled as usual.

Conclusion

Organisation for effective teaching and learning must be flexible. It is about compromise. Some of the teaching will be individual and some in small groups; sometimes it will be grouped according to interest, sometimes to ability, sometimes to a theme; sometimes there will be a class group, sometimes the organisation will be fully integrated and sometimes it will be only partially integrated, depending on what is appropriate to the demands of the task and the teaching and learning needs at the time. Teachers should ask themselves what it is they hope children will learn over a particular period. What are the experiences that will be provided? Which concepts, skills and attitudes are they hoping children will acquire? What developments in children's thinking are they expecting to occur? When they have the answers, they can organise in the most appropriate way. This is organisation being the servant, not the master. All debate about integrated or differentiated approaches, open-plan schools, vertical grouping, etc. is wasted unless the child learns better and with enjoyment. As far as possible he should achieve his competence level and develop effective thinking and feeling, together with a positive attitude towards learning.

References

Brearley M 1972 *Fundamentals in the First School.* Blackwell
DES 1985 *Better Schools.* HMSO
DES 1985 *Education Observed 3 - Good Teachers.* HMSO
DES 1987 *Primary Schools - Some Aspects of Good Practice.* HMSO
Humberside LEA 1986 *The School Curriculum in Humberside*
Smith F 1971 *Understanding Reading.* Holt, Rinehart, Winston
Taylor J 1983 *Organising and Integrating the First School Day.* Unwin

Further reading

Boydell D 1978 *The Primary Teacher in Action.* Open Books
Schools Council 1983 *Primary Practice - Working Paper 75.* Methuen

2   The management of collaborative teaching

Heather Toynbee

The historical background

In the past it was quite usual for class teachers to have almost complete autonomy over the way their rooms were organized, the resources that were provided in them and the curriculum to which their pupils were exposed. This led to lack of continuity throughout a child's time even in one school – for instance, one method of subtraction could be taught in one educational year and another in the next; and the same project could be tackled several times by different teachers, with little thought for progression in skills and content.

Headteachers often devolved their responsibility for buying books and equipment by allocating a lump sum to each member of staff. Goods thus ordered became in the class teachers' eyes their, rather than the school's, possessions. This led to a further lack of continuity and much duplication of resources. Vestiges of such a system still remain today, and throughout the years the opposition of teachers from such an era to a move towards a more cooperative approach has held back many progressive initiatives on the part of new or established senior staff.

Indeed, in DES (1982) it is stated that '... in 45 (out of the eighty first schools surveyed in England) there was either no explicit policy or it was believed that each teacher should determine his or her own classroom organisation and approaches to teaching'. HMI went on to comment 'Some decisions should properly be in the hands of individual teachers but complete freedom of choice can be counterproductive. Extreme changes of practice from one teacher to the next are, at best, temporarily disconcerting for children, and it is wise to adopt a framework of common practice'. Subsequent publications, for instance, DES (1985a) and DES (1985b) have all promoted a corporate and coherent approach to curriculum planning.

Unfortunately, the profession continues to be somewhat conservative, and present-day teachers, too, may well have been pupils who fared well in a traditional environment. Their inability to adopt a more open, flexible approach to the sharing of curriculum planning, classroom space and resources presents a continuing constraint in many schools. To work together requires a skill in communicating and coping with contention, which in the past was not required.

There certainly would seem to be a need for some reappraisal of teacher training methods to overcome this problem at source in order to dispel the assumption that the *modus operandi* of cooperation used in 'open plan' schools is pertinent to these alone, whereas all should be working towards such an approach whatever the type of building.

Pluckrose (1975) comments that:

> A number of headteachers have expressed surprise that, on transfer to a new building, it was the older teachers who adapted more easily to a 'new' teaching style rather than the young teachers straight from college . . . In a more open environment the teacher who succeeds will be the one who can fail, be seen to fail and yet not be undermined by failure, and who, in another context, can succeed; be seen to succeed and not be made complacent by success.

In all fairness, in a traditional, classroom-based school, it was seldom possible for one member of staff to see another in action, and it was difficult to instigate flexible groupings of children for different activities, even if the staff had so wished.

In no way were these bad teachers – many had interesting, well-organized classrooms – but the stress already placed in the Plowden Report (1967) on the need for a more professional and corporate approach had had little effect.

The part played by buildings in the management of collaborative teaching

Although innovative schools which broke with tradition had been built immediately after 1945, the classroom system, although different in character, held firm until the 1960s, when new open plan buildings became the norm in many authorities. However, many were built without much collaboration and understanding between designers and those who were advising and preparing teachers to work in them.

Early run of the mill open plan schools did at least have the advantage of space, and they have become even more workable in a falling roll situation. More contemporary buildings, owing to cost limits and government building regulations, are not so well endowed. Indeed, areas which were designated for circulation are now assessed as part of the teaching space. There is still much to be learnt before the ideal school is designed. To the philosopher and broadcaster Jacob Bronowski is attributed the remark 'A building is not a beautiful shell, and neither is it a functional shed. A building is a coherent solution to a problem of living.'

Dean (1984) said of the introduction of open-plan schools:

> One aspect of open plan schools and team teaching which I certainly did not appreciate fifteen years ago was the human need for territory which is defined. Looking back I can now see that one of the things which was most difficult for teachers was no longer knowing where your own territory lay ... I am very critical, with hindsight, of how little we did to prepare teachers for these new buildings.

This problem is still with us today, and there are many teachers thrown, sometimes without choice, into a situation in which the philosophy and way of working is quite different from their own. The outcome is that teachers are driven to barricade themselves into a defined area, thus defeating the intended objective of the building. This can be seen in schools up and down the country today.

A great deal of in-service support and management skill on the part of the headteacher and other senior members of staff is needed in such a situation, particularly where a new extension or refurbishment has altered the former organizational pattern of a school.

The influence of the headteacher

In the 1970s, several charismatic headteachers emerged, all advocating their own brand of team teaching – Arthur Razzell at Ravenscote Middle School in Surrey, Frank Plimmer at Great Hollands Junior School in Berkshire and Henry Pluckrose in London, for instance. These were prime exemplifications of the fact that it is the head's own philosophy, regardless of outside factors, age, background, type of school and so on, which is the main influence shaping the curriculum.

All these headteachers exhibited very different styles of management and leadership, but all had the ability to inspire staff to work in a cooperative way. Many of their acolytes went on to spread the 'gospel' still further, and there are many advisers and headteachers today whose educational thinking was initially shaped as a teacher in one of these schools. Such headteachers were able not only to influence the minds of those who worked with them, but also to affect irreversibly what those who worked with them felt about the educational needs of children. There is a great difference between those with traditional views and those influenced by the new thinking, and most schools will have teachers in each of the camps. Those in the latter are worth their weight in gold to new-style headteachers, for there is no need for explicit instructions to be given to them; they have implicit understanding of the philosophy which they strive to promote. Not all headteachers, even if they were capable of the same magnetic leadership, would wish to emulate the management styles of the pioneers. A more contemporary, collegiate approach is required today.

Towards a collaborative approach

On the arrival of a new headteacher or senior member of staff, many schools have radically to change direction towards a more collaborative approach. This often involves the support of the advisory team, plus the introduction, as vacancies occur, of new teachers of a similar philosophy. In such a situation it would be wise if changes were introduced slowly but progressively, with staff being set both short- and long-term attainable targets.

How can teachers who fear opening up be assisted to overcome this emotion? It helps to emphasize that they have much to share with other members of staff. When confidence is established, support in weaker areas can be mooted. This could be in the following forms: offering help from another teacher in the same school, pointing out and making attendance possible on suitable courses, arranging visits to other schools to see good practice, acquiring new equipment, or suggesting helpful reading materials.

The recent report, DES (1987), in which one of the themes was that of coordination, does not suggest that each area of the primary curriculum should be taught by a specialist teacher, but it does state that support can be given 'by having a colleague nearby to turn to for information and help and especially so if the roles of advisor and advised could be exchanged on other occasions so there is no question of hierarchy'. This course of action was also advanced in DES (1982) in which is stated:

Few teachers are expert in all parts of the curriculum. It becomes increasingly difficult for an individual teacher to provide the width and depth of all the work required to be taught to the older children and to cover a curriculum that requires, for example, more work in science, history and geography. The necessary help, support and advice may in part be given by heads and local advisers. It may also be provided by other teachers on the staff who have a special interest, enthusiasm and responsibility for a part of the curriculum and who act as consultants. Such teachers may give support in a variety of ways: by producing guidelines and schemes of work; by leading discussions and organising study groups; by disseminating work done on in-service courses; by working alongside class teachers; by assembling and organising resources; and occasionally by teaching classes other than their own.

Even in the most traditional building the growing sophistication and complexity of equipment and teaching skills implies a basic flexibility. This allows a degree of movement by children between one member of staff and another, and also means there is a need for members of staff to act as curriculum coordinators or consultants converting their own, and outside knowledge, into something used by the whole school.

In every type of school a cooperative approach can have great benefits, not the least of which are the following:

(a) Economy of materials and equipment, which can be centrally stored and used by all the staff.

(b) The most efficient use of human resources.

(c) The structuring into the system of the interests, enthusiasms and expertise of individual members of staff.

(d) A tailoring of content and approach which can be made to fit the needs of all the pupils.

(e) A framework within which subject integration can more easily take place.

(f) A good bridge between primary and secondary, i.e. the close-knit school community and the more impersonal school world.

(g) A way of involving the classroom teacher more actively and directly with the evolution of a meaningful curriculum.

(h) A way of taking the teacher away from the traditional isolation of the classroom.

(i) Continuous support from one's colleagues.

(j) A replacement of the traditional 'syllabus' with the continuous seminar in which all participate – a constantly evolving curriculum, a continuous creation.

(k) The opportunity to establish a resource centre or centres upon which all members of the staff can draw.

(l) An opportunity to place the needs of the individual child above those of the curriculum area, the constraints of the building, and lack of expertise on the part of any one member of staff.

Stress related to corporate planning

It must be remembered that stress can be experienced by teachers involved in corporate planning coupled with curriculum development, and both, of course, make considerable demands on teachers' time. If these are to be carried out successfully and sustained over a number of years, then there must be 'time' for such planning to be built into the organization of the school. In the past this has often been gained by headteachers taking on a heavy teaching commitment. In small schools, where the head might also be a class teacher, this has been well nigh impossible.

It is interesting to note that when Keith Joseph was in office he said that 15,000 more teachers were needed to provide the flexibility needed for corporate planning and curriculum development.

Many teachers see a lower pupil : teacher ratio only in terms of smaller classes. They need to ask themselves if this is the most valuable way for teaching hours gained to be used.

Fortunately the introduction of GRIST has at last made planning and development more available to all. This is Grant Related In-Service Training, which is funded by the DES and allows for schoolbased/focused schemes to take place, including the provision of supply teachers to release permanent staff for short periods in order to carry out their internal work as curriculum coordinators/consultants.

Collaborative planning in a traditional school

Senior staff would do well to remember that should an innovative idea fail, it will be doubly difficult to introduce the next one. A case of 'one step forward and two steps back' will undoubtedly result. Success, however small, should always be ensured in order to inspire confidence, not only in the teachers' capabilities, but also in the management skills of those involved. In a good class-based school there still can be much corporate planning which is pertinent to the whole, to parallel classes and to other groupings. The overall philosophy and aims and objectives, against which to judge the effectiveness of the school's work, can be formulated.

Guidelines can be produced together for the key areas of the curriculum, bearing in mind any relevant LEA documents and current educational thinking. Starting points might be defined, and discussion and practical sessions led, by the headteacher, but more often by a member of staff with a special responsibility. Not only will these sessions include consideration of content, but there should also be in-built progression and structure in skills and concepts. The needs of individual children will be taken into account, and the best use of resources – human and material – and the most efficacious use of the building considered.

There will be discussion and documentation, too, on the hidden areas of the curriculum in order to present a united front and establish uniformity. These might cover ways of dealing with indiscipline, classroom organization, acceptable social attitudes on the part of adults and children, record keeping, marking, presentation of work, display, evaluation, appraisal procedures, and so on. In the future, school development plans will be prepared by staff in conjunction with the governors.

Various schools overcome the problem of box-like classrooms in different ways – setting, designation of classrooms as workshops for particular areas of the curriculum, and the exchange of classes for various subjects are just three examples.

The complexities are endless, and it would be difficult to explain all the variations, which owe much to the ingenuity of headteachers and staff alike when they work together to overcome the constraints of a building. Under the direction of a good management team, all staff should grow in professional stature, and become able to put over their own informed points of view with self-confidence at staff meetings. They should be able to cope with criticism and compromise, and learn that conflict need not lead to rancour but should become an enlightening experience.

Managing collaborative teaching

An open-plan building presents many possibilities in the organization of cooperative teaching, and, of course, all the previous collaborative exercises mentioned in connection with a traditional building still pertain.

In the box-like classroom one teacher must provide all the stimulus and opportunities needed to match the abilities of thirty or so children. A team situation, with several teachers working together and with specialist areas in accessible reach, makes the setting of an appropriate broad, relevant, balanced and differentiated curriculum, as envisaged in DES (1985a) more of a possibility.

The building

In an open-plan school there are carpeted areas for quiet activities, some of which may be capable of being shut off by doors or partitions. These are usually used as home base areas. Within easy access there will be library facilities and areas furnished with sinks and non-slip flooring suitable for the noisier, messier activities. Because of the barn-like structure of some designs it is difficult for some practical work, such as music and woodwork, to take place without distracting others engrossed in quieter assignments, and staff would do well to consider using enclosed areas for these activities. In fact, some schools have turned their buildings inside out, and now utilize the more shut-in peripheral home bases as the noisy areas and the core, open area for quiet activities.

Another way of ensuring that there is an oasis of calm for at least some time during the week is to designate periods for silent reading. It must be ensured that there are no interruptions on these occasions – no messages from the office, no visitors – and that teachers and children alike enjoy reading and looking at books during this time.

To make best use of all the facilities, and to allow children the flexibility needed to produce work of quality, it is advisable that formal timetabling be kept to a minimum. However, where there is shared use of the hall and field, then obviously periods have to be allocated. This need not be for individual classes; it could be for teams. This allows for 'lead' lessons to be held, visiting speakers to be accommodated and so on, whilst making sure that every child has an adequate amount of physical exercise.

In primary schools where there are both infants and juniors, architects have not always recognized the efficacy of having the full age range in close proximity, and have designed two 'wings' with a buffer in between containing the hall, offices and staffroom. This is a great pity; staff must work to make sure that a continuum exists through all age groups, and that the school does not fall into two, or more, camps. This matter should be given prominent priority at senior management meetings and ways and means of breaking down such a 'divide' should be built into a school's organization in such circumstances.

Management teams

Schools often have a senior management team, comprising headteacher, deputy and team group leaders. This facilitates the work of the headteacher, as it involves negotiations with fewer people on top management issues and gives a line of communication for team members through their senior staff member. Such representatious obviously carry more weight, and are more persuasive, as they embody the opinion of groups rather than of individuals. It is important that the system reflects a measure of discussion and collaboration between members of a team.

A team leader exists to ensure smooth organization and a degree of leadership for both children and staff. She keeps an overview of what is happening in a team, and is the prime mover of change and adaptation to new ideas or improved practices. This does not preclude suggestions from other members regarding innovative initiatives upon which they might have a worthwhile influence.

The team leaders also liaise with other senior staff to ensure progression in educational practice and maintenance of the school's ethos and philosophy in their particular areas of the building.

A team can usually sort out its own differences, and this is the best way, but occasionally the headteacher or a member of senior staff has to step in as an arbitrator where a situation has got out of hand.

The dynamics of a team

When appointing people to collaborative teams it is advisable not only to strive for a mix of expertise but to look at the personalities involved. Teams are rather like marriages; some are wonderful, some just rub along, some are made in hell. Wise is the headteacher who at the end of a school year gives consideration to a new permutation which will eliminate the third category. T-group residential courses have been held in the past in order for team leaders to realize what the dynamics of a group of people working together in close proximity are. Being shut in a room under controlled conditions for almost a week with nine or ten colleagues soon reproduced, if in a highly accentuated form, many of the attributes of such a school section – it revealed the people who acted as conciliators, the ones who supported each other, those who opted out and those who sought to aggravate every situation. Everyone's little mannerisms became more and more annoying as time passed.

It is just like that, if to a lesser degree, in a team; often it is the staple-gun, put back in its box in an unusable condition, which is the catalyst for an eruption rather than any deep educational disagreement.

However, team teaching allows great support for established and new teachers alike, for no member of staff is ever on her own. Everyone learns from working together with others, and weaknesses can be corrected and attitudes changed more effectively than in a traditional classroom situation. On the other hand, a certain amount of autonomy is lost. Some teachers find it difficult to come to terms with this situation at the beginning; some never achieve that at all.

Team teaching facilitates the assimilation of supply teachers into a school making sure that there is a continuum during the absence of a permanent member of staff, and the work of peripatetic teachers of children requiring remedial assistance can be appropriately integrated. Also, it is easier for helpers – parents, friends, students and the like – to work with groups without disruption to the general organization pattern. New teachers, who have not been exposed to initial thinking and compilation of guidelines, can be inducted into the ways of the school by existing staff.

Care must be taken to see that the organization of the school is not so tight as to exclude newcomers from bringing with them interests and expertise which can freshen educational thinking throughout the school.

Senior staff should endeavour to continue to promote a climate which fosters and develops innovation not only in the pupils, but also in adults.

The organizational pattern

Instead of being in a class, children are often attached to a home base in a team situation; there they might have a pastoral teacher for only part of a day, and work on an assignment basis with two or three other members of staff for the rest of the time. There may be setting for a particular subject, usually mathematics. In some organizations teachers remain static in a particular curriculum workshop for one week or longer, and the children move from one to another.

One of the greatest advantages is that groupings of children can be of a flexible size – a lead lesson can be given to a whole team of, say, 100 or more, or a story can be read to two classes, whilst pupils requiring special attention can be seen in twos and threes.

Obviously much planning is needed, both day-to-day as well as long-term, and frequent informal meetings between the staff involved are a necessity. In such a situation where teachers are less instructors and more consultants, a great deal of individual and group work has to be organized, resources found, equipment prepared and so on. However, many hands make light work, and the pooling of ideas and the sharing of various tasks can in the end be less consuming of time than a traditional classroom approach.

In spite of the hard work entailed, and the fact that a member of staff seldom remains static but is constantly on the move over a wide area from one individual child to another or to a group of children, teachers, once they have successfully tried team teaching, rarely want to go back to classwork again. There might be times when everyone has a strong desire for a door to close and retreat behind, but these are easily offset by the days when everything is going well and the camaraderie of staff and children alike is uplifting.

Unfortunately, as I said earlier, many open-plan schools are still used in a much too inflexible way, which completely defeats the object of their original design. Some common pitfalls are:

(a) Attempts to give children a place of their own, which often leads to too much furniture being accommodated in too small a space.
(b) Too little use of practical areas at certain times of the day, especially the morning. To maximize space, all the areas should be in use for almost all the time.
(c) Too much directed, didactic work, which again holds children in defined areas when they should be allowed to move freely to collect equipment, make choices about materials and, to some extent, plan their own, self-motivated, day.
(d) Non-availability of materials, which leads to waste of time and frustration. Forward planning should ensure that all necessary resources are readily at hand and in a fit condition for use.

Unless these are strictly avoided the result for the teachers and the children can be disastrous. Staff working in a cooperative way must ensure that the open-ness is preserved, but that it is also carefully structured, according to criteria developed on a whole staff basis: otherwise the organization is likely to deserve the sort of criticism met with in Bennett's (1980) and Galton's *et al.* (1980) research projects.

The curriculum

In many schools, both traditional and open-plan, the majority of the curriculum is encompassed by an integrated studies project. Sometimes this is tackled on a team basis, sometimes the whole school participates at levels appropriate to the different age groups.

In order to achieve depth, there may be an emphasis on one particular area of the curriculum which is identified for inclusion in each project, e.g. science, history, craft/design/technology; and breadth and balance will occur over a longer period, as promoted in DES (1985b). This does not preclude the introduction of other subjects in the topic work at a more subsidiary level.

There is a need for some computational mathematics to be taught separately in order to ensure progression, but much of this subject can be integrated, and thus given more direct relevance.

The conventions of grammar and spelling can, in the main, be taught through the pupils' own writing. Older children should be given time to draft, and re-draft, their written work in order that corrections can be made, both by themselves and with the help of a teacher.

In recent years there has been a move towards children making illustrated 'books' of their work instead of using loose-leaf paper or exercise books. Good presentation, including handwriting, certainly improves the quality of the content, and this is an initiative well worth considering, but it should be taken on board by the whole school and not in a piecemeal fashion. Areas to be covered by each project should be considered well in advance by all members of staff involved. A brainstorming session is a good way of pooling ideas. The skills and concepts, as well as the content, that it is the aim to promote should be identified and flowcharts prepared showing how the work could be developed. Resources – project collections of books, museum loans and new equipment – appropriate visits and outside speakers can be arranged cooperatively.

At the end of each project a collaborative evaluation should be prepared, together with some form of overall record keeping showing what has been achieved.

Conclusion

In conclusion, I can only reiterate that outside forces now demand tangible proof of cooperation in the planning and implementation of the curriculum and this excludes any avenue for opting out by teachers.

If primary schools in the past had put their own houses in order, and not allowed a *laissez-faire* approach to prevail, then today we would not be facing the prescription of the core curriculum and other similar government measures. It is to be hoped that teachers can now assimilate these new initiatives and, having done so, will continue to work in the best way possible to meet the needs of each individual child, which can only be achieved by cooperation and collaboration on the part of teachers.

References

Bennett N (*et al.*) 1980 *Open Plan Schools: Teaching, Curriculum, Design.* NFER Publishing Company for the Schools Council

Dean J 1984 Yesterday's vision and today's practice. Transcript of talk to Open Plan Primary School Conference, Wokingham Teachers' Centre, Berkshire

DES 1967 *Children in Their Primary Schools* (The Plowden Report). HMSO

DES 1982 *Education 5 to 9: an Illustrative Survey of 80 First Schools in England.* HMSO

DES 1985a *Better Schools.* HMSO

DES 1985b *The Curriculum from 5 to 16.* HMSO

DES 1987 *Achievement in Primary Schools: the Select Committee's Report.* HMSO

Galton M, Simon B, Croll P 1980 *Inside the Primary Classroom (The Oracle Project)*. Routledge and Kegan Paul
Pluckrose H 1975 *Open School: Open Society.* Evans Brothers Ltd

3 Celebrating the vertically grouped class

John Barrett

'You see I'm lucky, I've got two-year groups in my class'. These were the words of a deputy headteacher of a large junior school as she addressed some teachers on a course. It is the sentiment behind these words that underpins the success of that teacher's class and indeed of his school. He was not describing an inherited circumstance or one endured through no other choice, but the result of a conscious decision taken in pursuit of a clear and shared purpose. There are many schools that do not enjoy the luxury of exercising such choice and for some the mixed-age group represents a frustration and a constraint.

This chapter contends that there is a considerable benefit in vertical grouping for both the child and the teacher, but does so on the following assumptions:

- That no matter how excellent an organisational model may appear on paper, unless those that are to implement it feel sympathy for it there will undoubtedly be a shortfall in what it might otherwise fulfil. It does not, of course, simply require compliance or even general sympathy, but the sustained commitment of reflective teachers.
- That the model adopted must be in the service of a shared and clearly articulated purpose.
- That the principles that underpin that purpose need periodically to be critically reviewed.
- That an essential need is to develop a reflective quality in which experience translates itself into growth.
- That the over-riding concern of schools is for the development of the individual and that the company in which children, as social beings, are variously placed will have a profound effect on their development.

There is no single way of grouping human beings that will prove satisfactory and productive in every detail for achieving a complex purpose. The human dimension is too complex for that to be the case. What must be striven for is a grouping that offers the optimum conditions to realise that agreed purpose.

Teaching well is a demanding and difficult task. It is proper and reasonable to seek means of reducing the difficulties for the teacher but not to the point of affecting the natural development of the children or their rate of progress. Where that point lies is clearly open to debate. One of the difficulties in such debate is that by nature the profession is somewhat conservative. Allied to this is the limited opportunity to stand back for any sustained period to review and reflect on what is an all-consuming and very sizeable task. This combination of constraints makes it difficult not to fall back on and rehearse familiar and perhaps comfortable arguments. The review of the arrangements for grouping children tends to be undertaken only when change in numbers makes it necessary and attitudes on this theme tend to be shaped by the patterns of tradition rather than by dispassionate analysis.

It is important to acknowledge that there has been adverse comment on vertical grouping. The HMI primary survey (DES, 1978) reported that 11-year-olds and to a lesser extent 9-year-olds in single-age classes produced better NFER scores for reading and mathematics than children in mixed-age classes. However, Galton and Simon (1980) and Marshall (1985) in Canada failed to find any significant difference. Even so, what might be judged a tendency does not determine that it has to be the rule, particularly bearing in mind that vertical grouping is often adopted through necessity and perhaps reluctantly rather than for its inherent merits. In any event, to gain a true picture of any organisational structure it must surely be necessary to measure more broadly.

Integration

Schools are principally concerned with teaching and learning. It is therefore necessary for each school to articulate its aims as learning outcomes. It cannot achieve these outcomes, however, without a clear understanding of the manner and circumstances in which children most readily learn. It is at this point that the issue of integration, both curriculum integration and social integration, becomes an important one. Though separate strategies they spring from the same pedagogical position, which sees learning as a natural phenomenon and seeks to adopt the natural learning characteristics in children's formal education.

Curriculum integration

Learning is a fundamental characteristic of the human being; it is a natural phenomenon. Children fuelled by their inherent energy and curiosity have an in-built learning appetite and it is life itself that provides the raw material for their learning. They learn by experiencing elements of the real world, synthesising their own knowledge through their experiences. The wider the range of those experiences the wider the range and depth of the skills required. The child's view of the world is fresh, questioning and uninhibited. It is unencumbered with the adult's retrospective view of learning. It seems a sensible and logical response to adopt children's view and perspective of the world as vehicles for their learning. Their preoccupations and passions can guide the teacher's planning. This is not a 'do what you like' approach but a skill in teaching which coopts the energy and concerns of children in the service of their own development. It is very much concerned with differentiation, progression and relevance, and does not obstruct the responsibility for balance.

Children's play is broken and changed informally. The patterns and rhythms of their play are governed by natural disciplines: concentration spans, depth of interest and alternative attractions. Children's impulses drive them to be doing. It is their spontaneous way of taking their world in and their natural means of growth. Their learning, however, is not simply active; it is collaborative and relies heavily on social interaction.

It seems hardly surprising, therefore, that where teachers' practice is informed and guided by sensitive observation of children they find themselves engaged in what has become known as the integrated day. It is the natural and inevitable consequence of children being involved in tasks that interest and engage them in a serious way and at levels commensurate with their learning capabilities.

If it is important to be guided by the natural behaviour of children in arranging their learning, so too must it be taken into account in arranging the circumstances for their learning.

Social integration

Grouping of children in single-year groups has long been the practice where numbers and staffing permit. The question that is being posed in this chapter is whether this is in fact the best possible learning circumstance that can be chosen, or whether it is continued more because it represents what has been inherited and become familiar.

The practice of streaming in schools has been largely set aside, based as it was on false psychological premises. Single-sex schools too have almost disappeared in the state primary sector, amongst other things in recognition of the fact that experience of life now is the best possible preparation for life as it really is. There is increasing integration of children with varying handicaps for much the same reason. The integration of children of different ages also deserves scrutiny.

Is it necessary to break the pattern of the learning circumstance that is experienced in the family and wider society? In both of those areas there is very considerable integration. It could be argued that the process of 'integration' has only become necessary now because learning and grouping were disintegrated in the first place. To put children in groups of mixed ability, age and sex is to simulate the normal circumstances of life itself. Such a grouping is akin to the experience a child brings to school. It is, like a family, a mixed society but it is on a larger scale.

The family provides the most natural social group for a child to develop and grow in. It is founded in love. It enjoys a flexibility of social relationships and offers a pattern for living and learning. It is the base from which children explore and become increasingly involved in their world. The success of these excursions will rest heavily on the child's sense of social and emotional security. Relationships with other children form a vital part of their daily lives and it is significant that when there is a range of options of companionship available, the age factor is by no means a dominant one. This is hardly surprising, bearing in mind the very considerable differences in physical, emotional and intellectual development of children of the same age.

The family has proved to be a very successful agent of learning and learning is a continuum, it does not begin at 5. However, interposed between children's early years, closely tied to the family, and their later years as adults in the wider society, comes school. It is a commonly held view that life and learning are synonymous; that learning is in fact a life-long process. We are perhaps in danger of undermining that understanding in the very organisational structures we create. We send our children 'to learn' between particular hours of the day, on certain days of the year and in a special building. We arrange them in most instances in groups of similar age and may expect them to wear particular clothes in which 'to learn'. Their learning often arises from books with scant relation to the reality of their own experience.

What are the implicit conclusions to be drawn by children about what school is, as a consequence of their experience in it? The need for planning and organisation is, of course, not being challenged. It is simply worth reflecting on the form, style and effect of the learning experiences and the organisational structures we employ. It is the integrity of both curriculum and organisational divisions that is being explored.

Vertical grouping

The child in joining a vertically grouped class becomes a member of an established group with established codes and patterns of work and a sense of stability, tradition and security. At best it is simply a larger family. The teacher in that arrangement has, of course, fewer children to get to know and is aided in that process by the tradition of the class and the momentum it provides. The older children are capable not only of pursuing their own work and thus freeing the teacher in the early days of the term but also of sharing in the responsibility for receiving, welcoming and supporting the new children. This view was reinforced by a teacher working in a junior school when she moved from the upper juniors to the lower juniors: 'I had forgotten just how hard it is to start from scratch with a whole class'.

There is, of course, more to it than mere simulation of life outside school. A fundamental role of education is to develop and refine the capacity and appetite children have for learning. It seeks to foster the foundation of life-long habits and attitudes towards learning. There can be no better company in which to learn than that of those who by the benefit of greater experience are further along the road. Quite apart from any deliberate teaching there is a half-conscious absorption of knowledge and attitudes drawn from the experience of just being with older children.

The imitative process is a powerful and natural learning agent. This is clearly observed in children's play. Though a further educational responsibility is to promote independence and self-reliance, the process of imitation is one that is never entirely discarded. Such fundamental learning characteristics should be coopted in the organisational structures of the school. This is particularly fostered by the nature of the primary classroom.

The classroom in a primary school is an environment offering stimulation and challenge. It is a workshop which is part studio, part library and part laboratory. It is in effect a place of action, very public action. To join a group already practised and more accomplished in its use, which knows what tools are available, how they are used and where they are kept and which has established a work ethic, is simply to capitalise on children's capacity to learn from those about them. The new year begins as a going concern. New class members absorb what it has to offer. There is a natural transmission of skills, attitudes and knowledge.

Comment so far has been concerned with the younger children. There are, of course, the needs of the older children to consider. What is their gain from such an arrangement? In the first place, they benefit from being in the company of a teacher who can draw on an all-round knowledge of them. It is in the context of such understanding that wise decisions are made on their behalf, decisions that are informed by at least a year's shared experiences. It seems an unnecessary squandering of an established rapport to transfer more than is necessary. Children are more likely to grow to the full in an environment that encourages growth and the quality of the relationships is probably the most fundamental of all influences. It is a strong and stable relationship with a teacher built over a considerable period that provides the most favourable of learning circumstances. There is an openness and trust that allows for real issues to be confronted, for the taking of risks and for experimentation. It is, of course, true that such an arrangement can be made with single-year groups simply by the teacher moving up with the children. Experience suggests, however, that this is a strategy that is rarely employed.

To know a child well must also mean knowing the parents. The notion of the parent–teacher partnership is given greater credence in that it has a more realistic period of time to become established. There is not a complete set of parents to get to know each September. The sense of shared enterprise between teacher, child and parent in which all feel they have a genuine stake is genuinely enhanced.

There is as well the opportunity for the older children to be the pace-setters, to provide the model as they go about their work for the younger children. They can be the helpers, the supporters, the demonstrators and teachers. The value of playing such roles should not be under-estimated. It heightens self-esteem, it can consolidate partly-formed skills and concepts; part of the process of explaining to others is the re-examination and confirmation of what is already known or half-known. It is a very natural and important function in life, a skill that can only be developed through purposeful use. None of these factors precludes children from working hard at their own intellectual level. The vertically grouped class can offer considerable flexibility in the grouping of children. Groups are composed with teaching and learning purposes in mind. The composition and size of groups will vary in relation to those purposes. In one class the determinants of the composition of groups during a week's observation included an assessment of children who quite simply worked well together, a more able child with a less able or a rather excitable child with a calmer one. What is offered is an increased number of possibilities open to both teachers and children.

Experience also suggests that vertical grouping has the effect of tailoring the work more precisely to the needs and interests of the individual, which in turn simply increases the chance of stimulating interest and securing engagement on the part of the child. This heightens the chance of success and there is no more powerful and creative agent than that for development.

There are also benefits from the teacher's point of view. Irrespective of the age-range within a class, the responsibility for its well-being and smooth running does not fall wholly on the shoulders of the teacher. It should not feel as though 'there is just one of me and thirty of them'; rather that 'there are thirty-one of us'. A feeling of partnership should prevail. This should be an explicit expectation with an increasing understanding that to be a member of a community carries responsibilities. In any event, children need to develop an increasing autonomy, so that their thoughts and actions do not simply rely on instruction or reference to the influence of others. They require opportunity to exercise initiative, and to acquire a growing mastery of an increasing range of skills, the capacity to cope with and understand failure, and a confidence in their own ideas, feelings and capabilities. These are important life skills and can only be developed in their exercise.

Where those qualities of self-reliance exist and where a real sense of mutual support prevails teachers find themselves more able to observe. The need to 'police' and 'fire-fight', to be caught up in mundane routine, is diminished. Their teaching is guided more by sensitive observation than by mere force of habit. The class becomes not simply 'child-centred' but also 'teacher-centred'. The teacher's growth is facilitated as well as that of the children. It is in this climate that more measured judgement can be made; there is a reflective quality in the teaching and the wide variety of roles played by the teacher become more apparent: the encourager, the listener, the guide, the peacemaker, the sounding-board, the approver, the extender, the ally. The experience of today increasingly provides the shaping influence of tomorrow.

These qualities in themselves are not peculiar to vertical grouping, but in such a class they are easier to maintain. The physical, mental and emotional strain traditionally associated with the annual upheaval is radically reduced.

The curriculum and organisational structures as briefly explored have been arrived at by a string of natural and logical considerations. What is achieved in such arrangements is a reduction of artificiality and a closer accordance with natural learning characteristics.

Glimpses of vertical grouping in action

Preparation for transfer from infant to junior school

The process of development, whether intellectual, social or emotional, is one of adaptation and reorientation. It is a proper function of education to extend children's horizons but those horizons must have some familiar landmarks and be viewed with reasonable confidence. To fail to take into account the considerable emotional and social factors at the time of transfer is simply to deepen and prolong the sense of insecurity and in so doing to postpone any real development. It is in the effort to minimise anxiety that the following policies are employed in one particular junior school.

Half-way through each summer term each child due to transfer from the associated infant school receives a letter from one of the current first-year junior school children. The letter in itself implies welcome and provides the comforting knowledge to each child that they have been identified and acknowledged in their own right and that their arrival is warmly anticipated. It is interesting that this simple tradition is clearly valued by the children. This is not only commented on by the parents but is evident in the care and thought that one year later the children give to writing their own letters.

Junior school staff make a series of visits to see the children in the context of a familiar setting, to sit with them and share some good moments. A pleasant and happy shared experience is a powerful social welding agent. The new parents, of course, visit the junior school. It is important that all the people most closely involved in the child's life are seen to be fully informed, involved and, hopefully, happy about the impending transfer. The children themselves visit the school on two afternoons which they each spend in the company of the child who has written to them. On this occasion they generally choose something from the school museum's collection to draw and are likely to be given a book in which to try some handwriting patterns. They sit together and remind themselves of the story they had shared a few weeks earlier and enjoy another.

The arrival of the new children in September is staggered to ensure ease of welcome. In their new class they find their pictures carefully displayed on the wall and in their drawer they find their handwriting book. It is also previously arranged with them that they will bring something of special interest with them. This provides the focus for much of their work for the first few all-important days, to be undertaken with the support of the second-year 'friends'.

These activities are, of course, not being presented as revolutionary; they merely acknowledge that the degree of social and emotional stability strongly influences the capacity for intellectual growth and demonstrate how supportive the vertically grouped class can be in gaining this degree of security. The older children anticipate the arrival of the younger children with pleasure. Their own memories of their first day are not too distant to stir emotional memories. It requires little encouragement for them to play a supportive role; in some respects they are better equipped for it than the teacher. A comment frequently expressed by teachers experiencing vertical grouping for the first time is how much less inclined the children are to cling to them.

Many of the things that they need to know and many of the conventions and agreements that shape the well-being and the daily life of the school are learnt simply by being in the company of those that know them. The wish to conform at such a stage is a powerful one. An important determinant of a school's success lies in its ability to coopt such tendencies and it is a two-fold success; not only does it achieve its purpose, it lightens the load of the teacher.

Responding to individual needs

Philip, who had to cope with quite widespread difficulties as a first-year entrant, was both immature and very disorganised. On the first day of his second year his teacher returned to her class at ten minutes to nine to find him already engaged in a task. The transformation that this and other small incidents highlighted was very apparent to his teacher, but as she put it, 'Philip too must be aware of his growth; he must be able to see and feel the difference as contrasted against the new, younger and less experienced arrivals'. How important it is for him to be conscious of that gain, particularly as he continues to experience his earlier difficulties. How important it is for his teacher not merely to be reminded of that growth but also to have the opportunity to build on it and share that knowledge with him. It is the two-year age group that made that growth explicit to them both. Philip was not about to begin a new year and form a new relationship with another teacher. He had a history, he knew what it was and he knew that his teacher knew.

His teacher commented, 'last year Philip experienced doing a lot of things as a learner, this year he will experience doing things as an expert as well'. There were, indeed, to be a number of activities that Philip would be undertaking in the company of the younger children because it was appropriate for him to do so. The many social mixes that form and re-form, as determined by the task in hand and the varying demands it might make, ensured that the age factor was of no consequence. It attracted no stigma or remark. It was easy and inconspicuous for him to proceed at an appropriate level and pace. It also provided the circumstance for him to lead. In one instance, for example, he was able to help the younger children with their first piece of clay work; first to find the appropriate tools and to set their workspace up; then to teach them some fundamental skills; and in due course to show them how to clear away, wash the tools and deal with the unused clay. Philip's contribution was evidenced in their success and undoubtedly contributed to his growth in confidence.

His teacher acknowledged and valued the reduced sense of anxiety offered by this extended period together. 'I felt towards the end of Philip's first year I was just getting there. The chance of a second year with him took away that sense of panic, frustration and anxiety'. Freedom from the tension aroused by anxiety for both teacher and child simply enhances their chance of success.

The next example was also made possible by the hierarchical nature of the class. The teacher was employing the maturity and mathematical skills of Glen, a fourth-year boy, to help two third-year boys. Andrew and Lee, having undertaken some work on speed and distance involving children running over a given distance, now wanted to measure the speed of the traffic on the road running alongside the school. This was a matter of genuine interest to them, and indeed a subject for periodic discussion in the school as a whole because the road was becoming increasingly busy and the majority of children had to cross it daily. They had previously decided that they would send their findings to the police station.

The teacher reinforced in Glen's mind the need to keep the two younger boys on the task and to encourage accuracy. They had clearly benefitted from the previous task, which, for example, helped them to determine the distance over which to measure the cars, mindful of later calculations. The task was set up and undertaken, and the boys returned with their information recorded in a matrix. The presence of Glen had helped to ensure that the two somewhat excitable boys had completed the task properly and produced valid data on which to work. He then helped them in the calculation of the speeds.

In this task the learning arose from a natural consequence. There was no antipathy towards the use and development of skills; they had meaning and purpose. Investigating is an inherent activity. The teacher was exploiting both that and the available human resources.

The workplace

'We are all shareholders in this place', said the head of a village school. 'We've all got a stake in it and, anyway', she continued, 'they (the children) are the first to complain if tools and materials are not to hand'. This was a school with an established tradition of promoting children's personal autonomy and self-direction. In the practicalities of sharing a workshop this implied that the children themselves should be capable not just of using their workshop but of managing it too. 'A place for everything and everything in its place' was the agreement for the end of each day. A respect for tools and the unwillingness to tolerate waste were also well-established attitudes. The children knew about capitation and limited budgets. They also knew that the state of their workshop was a shared responsibility. Such attitudes are not established overnight nor indeed was the resourcing and physical organisation of the working environment.

Children learn through just being in the environment, through conditioning by direct experience, by observation, by being told, by listening and through being taught. Much of what is learnt is somehow accumulated; it is acquired, though precisely how it is often difficult to pinpoint. There is a process of integration by which children are drawn into a vertically grouped class until they become part of it. The organisation of the class slowly reveals itself to them. Clearly the need for a wide range of tools and materials and the ability to locate and use them provide the means of self-direction and autonomy. As the headteacher put it, 'it is not just because I believe this organisation offers an extremely efficient and effective way of learning, it has something to do with self-preservation as well!'. Where such an active and self-directed style is adopted, where there is a sense of cooperation and support and where children are able to exercise their initiative, the pace of the teacher's day becomes more relaxed and by inference more productive.

Conclusion

Teachers are regularly engaged in the process of assessing the successes and failures of the children they teach. It is the product of this assessment that provides the pointers for future development. An inevitable inclination, though, in making such assessment is to attribute failures to the children whereas it may well be that the curriculum, the teaching method, the climate in the school or the organisational structures should shoulder some of that responsibility. Each child possesses a potential, and it is the task of the school to create the most favourable circumstances it can to convert that potential into fulfilment. Peer group structure conventionally rests on the idea that if children are grouped by age then the members of that group will be sufficiently alike to ease resourcing and teaching. Yet the reality is that children learn at their own irregular and individual pace and the teacher is constantly adapting to individual needs. Children are a subtle mixture of differing abilities, aptitudes and experiences. Allied to that is the fact that the educational process is fundamentally a social exercise in which the learners are grouped in a manner that harnesses a variety of abilities, aptitudes and experiences towards a given purpose. The combination of these two factors suggests that the notion of peer groups for children in all their variability demands a more generous and flexible interpretation than simply age. It is vertical grouping that can contribute to this flexibility.

References

DES 1978 *Primary Education in England; a Survey by HM Inspectors of Schools.* HMSO

Galton M, Simon B 1980 *Inside the Primary Classroom.* Routledge and Kegan Paul

Marshall D G 1985 Closing small schools or when is small too small? *Education Canada* 10–16.

4 Balancing the curriculum

Tony Wainwright

We need balance in our life to ensure a healthy mind and body. Our eating habits, if regulated by a balanced and varied diet, should keep us in sound physical condition. Maintaining the balance between work and play keeps the pressures at a level we can cope with. As the old saying goes, 'variety is the spice of life', and we are all far more interesting people as a result of varied and rich experiences acquired over a period of time with the appropriate degree of balance than we would be without those experiences.

The range of experiences we offer to children in school we call the curriculum. This is their diet whilst they are with us in the classroom and the requirement for balance is just as important as in other aspects of life. This chapter is concerned with the question of balance between the various curriculum areas and examines the issues from the class teacher's point of view. Teachers are constantly hearing that they are accountable and they feel the pressures bearing down upon them from parents, governors, the DES and the LEA, all of whom would claim that they have considerable influence in what is taught and some say in evaluating the outcomes. In reality, the teachers are accountable to the children in their charge. If teacher's efforts are channelled towards meeting children's individual needs and giving each child the opportunity to maximise his potential, always encouraging progress rather than discouraging it, then the job is being well done. Other agencies will recognise this. The public at large need to be shown good primary practice in action and perhaps there is a need for our more able practitioners to put their goods on display more often.

The curriculum

The HMI series *The Curriculum from 5 to 16* lists nine areas of learning and experience which should combine to form the curriculum for all schools. These are as follows: aesthetic and creative, human and social, linguistic and literary, mathematical, moral, physical, scientific, spiritual and technological. Despite the fact that many of these areas are taught as separate subjects in some schools, they are not intended to be exclusively discrete elements and a feature of many real and meaningful learning experiences for children in the primary years has been the interdisciplinary approach in the planning of the work.

On occasion teachers have been over-concerned about providing an equal ration of each element in planning a work programme for children. Different topics lend themselves more to some curriculum areas than to others and it is pointless to include something simply to fulfil a requirement simply because it is within a structure which does not allow for flexibility. Whatever is included must be relevant and it needs to fit naturally into the other planned stages.

Children, however, have the right of access to a broad-based curriculum and, if they are to be afforded an opportunity to maximise their potential, they need to be given a fair share of each of the nine areas of learning and experience during their schooling. In the primary school this must be central to the school's curriculum policy. This broad base is directly linked to balance and is also concerned with vital planning issues such as continuity and progression, relevance, degree of match and evaluation. It is no longer acceptable for capable primary school teachers to do their own thing. The demand for structure is clearly with us and the schools that are successful in planning and implementing their policies are those where all the staff have been involved in the process of curriculum development.

Balancing the curriculum

Certain issues need careful consideration in ensuring curriculum balance. The nine areas referred to previously must each play their part in determining the range of the curriculum over a period of time. Each area does not stand in isolation and teachers need to give thought to a varied interdisciplinary mix in order to derive maximum benefit through effective learning experiences for the children. Each area of learning and experience might have an essential content element and key concepts that need to be explored. Care must be taken to ensure that these are complemented by a range of suitable informal activities. Opportunities for active learning and first-hand experience must play a vital part in structuring a curriculum programme. There are implications here for teaching styles. Within the prescribed balanced framework most teachers opt for a combination of didactic and exploratory methods. These were described as follows by HMI (DES, 1978):

> A didactic approach was one in which the teacher directed the children's work in accordance with relatively specific and predetermined intentions and where explanations usually, though not always, preceded the action taken by the children. An exploratory approach was one in which the broad objectives of the work were discussed with the children but where they were then put in a position of finding their own solutions to the problems posed and of making choices about the way in which the work should be tackled.

It is a worthwhile exercise for a teacher to reflect upon his approach with regard to balance in teaching approach. Some forward-thinking school staffs are now into the process of peer group classroom observation as part of their staff development programme. An interesting outcome of these exercises has been the different perceptions of styles identified by the performer and the observer.

Another factor affecting balance is that of pupil organisation. Basically there are three ways of doing this: treating the class as a whole unit, dividing it into groups of children and dealing with children as individuals. There are, of course, different ways of grouping. Certain tasks might require setting in ability groups, others are far more effectively undertaken by friendship groups; and the arrangement of children in small groups or in pairs is frequently seen by teachers as an effective method of achieving collaborative learning. It is worth noting, however, that the notion of pairing children does not necessarily mean that they are working together or indeed collaborating in any way. If effective collaboration is to be forthcoming, it is important that the pair understand the nature of the task before them and perceive the need to work together in order to achieve a successful outcome. This may well involve teacher intervention at an appropriate moment.

In short, in an endeavour to look for balance, a degree of flexibility in pupil grouping is desirable and will help to sustain interest for the children. The variety of experiences in terms of pupil interaction will provide a cornerstone within the framework for a broad-based, balanced curriculum.

Although they recognise the need for balance, many teachers become concerned with the notion that all integrated work should contain an equal portion of each curriculum area, and feel that otherwise an imbalance is evident. If a chef were planning menus for a given duration, he would not go to great lengths to ensure that each dish contained an equal share of a given number of ingredients. He should ensure, however, that the menus contained a sensible balance of ingredients, presented in different forms, over the prescribed period. In this way his customers would be presented with a varied and attractively presented choice, carefully selected for their enjoyment, nourishment and physical well-being. So it is with children. They need curriculum balance over time. The period of time may be a week, a half-term, a term or even a year. One theme may draw extensively from within some curriculum areas, another will rectify the balance at a later stage by drawing from others.

The balance cannot be achieved by chance. It is not good enough to review the curriculum late in the school year to see what has been missed out and to have an intensive attack on those areas in an attempt to restore the balance. There is a great need for structure. The curriculum framework for the school year should be planned in advance with balance in mind. More thorough short-term planning with careful monitoring should ensure that the parameters prescribed within the framework are not exceeded, and on-going evaluation should also ensure that the learning experiences for the children match the intended outcomes and that the curriculum balance is appropriate in meeting all their needs.

Pupil-initiated learning

It is important for children at times to be the agents in designing their learning activities. The teacher is the enabler, intervening at appropriate moments, but leaving the planning, to a large extent, to the children themselves.

An excellent example of this type of activity took place a few years ago in a village school in West Berkshire. The 10- and 11-year-olds formed the vertically grouped upper junior class and they were discussing their forthcoming social studies work with their teacher, who was also the headteacher. She was showing the class the original school log-book which dated back to mid-Victorian times, when the school had first opened. The children were extremely interested in the fortnightly test results entered in the meticulous copper-plate hand of the teacher, recording attainments in the test which had been administered by the school inspector. Two tests were set, one for arithmetic and one for spelling. Each test consisted of twenty questions. With encouragement from the teacher, the class decided to use the information in the log-book as source material for their half-term social studies project.

They began by developing their mathematics by using the test data. This involved the production of line graphs and histograms illustrating the progress of individual children and identifying areas of improvement or regression. They also worked out averages for everyone and calculated the mean score for the class. They compared the results with similar test scores of their own and, although the original test questions were not available, they realised that all the children, regardless of ability and attainment level, had been given the same test. This, they concluded, was not appropriate for all the children, as the test results clearly showed.

Two children, we will call them John Smith and Mary Brown, consistently scored 0 and 20 respectively and were the subject of further comments written in the log-book. John Smith was invariably caned for failing to register a correct answer. Frequently he attempted to absent himself on the day of the test, but usually turned up late with his irate mother and probably suffered two canings for his efforts. The children were incensed at the lack of sensitivity towards John Smith and discussed what help would be forthcoming if he had been in school now. The test level would have been appropriate to his ability, the teacher would have given him special attention, extra help might have been brought in from outside and perhaps other children would have taken turns in helping him catch up with the others. He certainly had their sympathy, and caning, they considered unanimously, was probably the most inappropriate solution to his problems.

Mary Brown got all her sums and spellings right and was the subject of some extremely complimentary remarks in the log-book. The children had mixed feelings about her and some decided she might have been 'a creep'. At the age of 11 she represented the school in a special test in the county town to write a composition for the annual Bishop's Prize, a gilt-edged bible. Mary duly won the prize and was recognised as the cleverest child in all the village schools in the area. Her own school were awarded an extra day's holiday by the managers and Mary was undoubtedly popular with her classmates as a result.

The present-day class discussed these two children at length and decided to trace their class further. They began by working in groups and predicting their respective paths. This led to some good imaginative writing. The only certain conclusion they reached was the fact that both people would now be dead (they were born about 1860). There was general agreement that John Smith may have fallen foul of the law. Nobody cared about him, apparently, so why should he bother about others? Would he have got a job? Did you need to read and write and do simple calculations in those times in order to survive and hold down an occupation? The general conclusion was that he probably had an unfortunate adult life and may well have spent time in prison, although the class hoped they were wrong and that his unfortunate home life and schooling had not had long-term adverse effects upon him.

Mary Brown would have gone on to some form of higher education, perhaps a university, although the children's research into this did not indicate a range of opportunities for further academic progress at that time. The final consensus view was that Mary probably became a teacher.

How were the children going to test their theories? Eventually they decided upon two sources, the parish records and the local archivist. Their efforts were rewarded and they discovered that their conclusion regarding John Smith had been sadly correct. He died in prison at the age of 29, having spent most of his adult life in custody for a series of minor offences, usually stealing. Mary Brown died at the age of 19 of consumption in her bed in the maidservants' quarters in the home of the Lord of the Manor. She had probably slept in a damp bed, a major factor in her physical deterioration. She became a maid because she was a working-class girl and this was her station in life, her social expectation.

There were tears in the eyes of the children when they discovered this. The discussion that followed was intense. Comparisons between now and then, further historical investigation, the advance of medical science, sociological conclusions, etc. brought about some superb language development, both verbal and written, and the effect it had in formulating attitudes was really quite marked. These children had been real agents in their own learning. The project had involved curriculum balance in respect of mathematical, human and social, linguistic, moral and scientific areas of learning and experience. It involved real collaborative learning and was extremely relevant. These children were all highly motivated and eager and ready for further developments. They didn't go home at night and say 'history is boring'.

Planning for balance

Preparation is the key to success. Working cooperatively with others provides the stimulus for effective thinking at the planning stage. It is often useful to commence with a brainstorming session where everyone concerned contributes any ideas that spring to mind. In planning for a particular project, with balance in mind, a flow chart can be a useful tool in establishing content. Listing activities relating to different disciplines around a central theme can be a simple starting point (Figure 4.1). The more sophisticated exercise in determining skills to be acquired, concepts to be understood and attitudes to be developed can follow later.

The project area having been decided upon, teachers then need to discuss possibilities for action, taking into account existing resources and other sources that might be available for obtaining materials for the project.

The planning of a topic with breadth and balance in mind is best exemplified by a real situation. A group of first school teachers in East Dorset worked together on the Cranborne Chase Project and planned an historical study for the children based upon the moot at Kingston Lacy, which was a medieval court where the Lord of the Manor held regular meetings with the villagers, collected taxes and administered justice. The project involved the children in a great deal of role play and a variety of ideas stemmed from the teachers in preparing a medieval topic through drama. This involved seven areas of learning and experience, integrated within the original theme, and linked the six schools involved through planned cooperative activities.

Balance within a curriculum area

Each area of learning and experience lends itself to the acquisition of a range of skills and different activities for children. Drama, for example, might range from the discipline of the annual school production where children are learning the principles of stagecraft to the free expression evident in role play where the children are playing with words, developing language and building up their self-confidence and self-esteem.

Figures 4.2, 4.3 and 4.4 show the planning technique used by a teacher in East Dorset who favours the use of matrices for this purpose. Weekly plans ensure a balance within each discipline as indicated.

A record of the work undertaken by the children is neatly made using these matrices and the programme can be passed on at the end of the year so that the next teacher can plan to ensure progression and continuity.

The same teacher took 'old things' as a topic for her class and planned the theme through an historical bias. A range of artefacts and documents were considered in ensuring balance and variety in the children's work (Figure 4.5).

The use of a matrix in planning work is a simple and effective instrument. It is easy to construct and easily understood by others. In looking for balance in planning a topic or in developing a curriculum area across a school it is helpful to plan each stage through the years, ensuring continuity and progression.

Figure 4.1 – An approach to an historical project within the first school

Language
Writing – in role of village characters and jousting knights. Instructions – traps – medicines – clamp kiln making – recall of moot day – meeting Lord of Manor. Feelings about visit to manor house. Reporting on visits. Researching through reference material.

Oral work – discussion in role – teaching another villager a craft/skill. Setting up individual village characters through role play. Reporting of events. Cooperative decision making in order to present grievances to Lord of Manor. Discussing medieval village life.

Religious education
Crusades. Joan of Arc. Feudal system – tithing. Justice and punishments. Morality.

Visual arts
Clay work – making money pots – clamp kiln fired – weaving – leather pouch – thonging – sketching manor house/artefacts – coats of arms – personally symbolic junk models – castles/gibbets/stocks/jousting props/ illustrative art – folders/costume research/papier mâché hogs – joint book making – flip-over books – string prints of knights in armour/class paint/collage work of medieval village. Creating costumes.

Environmental science
Comparison of diet. Cooking. Preserving. Coppicing. Wattling. Daubing. Observation of medieval structures. Building of clamp kiln. Porosity of pots. Study of medicine – use of herbs. Animals living locally – making and designing animal traps.

MEDIEVAL

TOPIC

THROUGH

DRAMA

Music
Creating medieval sounds, patterns and rhythms. Listening to medieval music – recorded by professional musicians. Researching and learning medieval music – composing lyrics – dancing bear music.

Mathematics
Money – barter – working out possible dates/systems mathematics from dates of kings' reigns. Time – looking backwards – time lines – telling the time. Relative values – wages/fines/dues/taxes. Medieval strategy games. Map making – direction and coordinates. Shape – problem-solving measurement – scale plan. Coins. 3D projection from ground plan of manor house. Weighing and estimating – investigation of weights of weaponry.

Science
Comparison of diet. Cooking. Preserving. Coppicing. Wattling. Daubing. Observation of medieval structures. Building of clamp kiln. Porosity of pots. Study of medicine – use of herbs. Animals living locally – making and designing animal traps.

Cooperative ventures
Fostering interaction – children/staff through children from different schools planning and sharing ideas. Staff exchanges to extend curriculum expertise, culminating in moot day re-enactment.

Figure 4.2 – Language project plan

Date	Personal writing Empathy Drama	Descriptive writing	Factual writing	Creative/ imaginative writing	Scientific writing Making hypotheses and predictions
Week 1					
Week 2					
Week 3					
Week 4					
Week 5					

Figure 4.3 – Mathematics/science project

Date	Shape/area	Capacity	Time	Weighing	Money	Measuring	Scientific investigations
Week 1							
Week 2							
Week 3							
Week 4							
Week 5							

Figure 4.4 – Art project

Date	Representation					Creative				
	Drawing	Print	Collage	Paint	3D	Drawing	Print	Collage	Paint	3D
Week 1										
Week 2										
Week 3										
Week 4										
Week 5										

Figure 4.5 – History-based topic plan

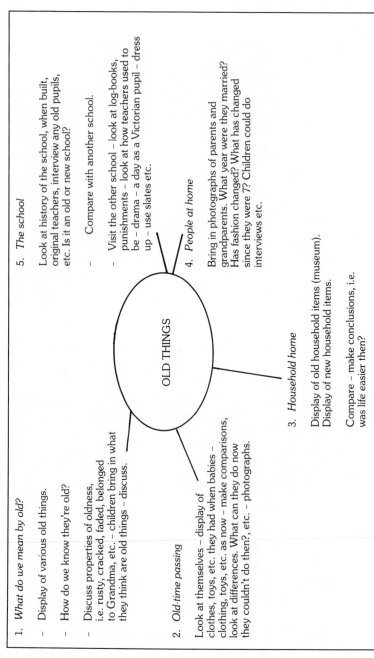

1. *What do we mean by old?*

   – Display of various old things.

   – How do we know they're old?

   – Discuss properties of oldness,
     i.e. rusty, cracked, faded, belonged
     to Grandma, etc. – children bring in what
     they think are old things – discuss.

2. *Old-time passing*

   Look at themselves – display of
   clothing, toys, etc. they had when babies –
   clothing, toys, etc. as now – make comparisons,
   look at differences. What can they do now
   they couldn't do then?, etc. – photographs.

OLD THINGS

3. *Household home*

   Display of old household items (museum).
   Display of new household items.

   Compare – make conclusions, i.e.
   was life easier then?

4. *People at home*

   Bring in photographs of parents and
   grandparents. What year were they married?
   Has fashion changed? What has changed
   since they were 7? Children could do
   interviews etc.

5. *The school*

   Look at history of the school, when built,
   original teachers, interview any old pupils,
   etc. Is it an old or new school?

   – Compare with another school.

   – Visit the other school – look at log-books,
     punishments – look at how teachers used to
     be – drama – a day as a Victorian pupil – dress
     up – use slates etc.

Figure 4.6 – Action plan

Topic title

Year	Themes to be explored	Activities	Resources available in school	Resources needed
1				
2				
3				
4				

Figure 4.7 – Curriculum development plan

Year	Topic title			
	Skills to be developed	Key concepts	Essential content	Subject balance
1				
2				
3				
4				

The matrices shown in Figures 4.6 and 4.7 cover both the practical resource requirement and plan for action and a consideration of the elements of learning required within the project. In considering the latter, teachers need to address the skills and seek a balance throughout the work in helping children to develop skills across a wide range. HMI in their curriculum matters series suggest the following eight groups of skills for development: communication, observation, study, problem solving, physical and practical, creative and imaginative, numerical and personal and social. With these in mind and a concentration upon progression, teachers can plan a cohesive well-balanced development throughout the years. Similarly, key concepts for children to encounter, identify and understand are again part of the development process across the four years with the level of understanding becoming higher as the children progress through the school. It is also important to consider essential content. It may be the intention for some knowledge to be acquired. This is quite acceptable providing it is relevant, understood by the children, worth knowing and provides a platform for further knowledge and understanding. Some of these conditions should be fulfilled, otherwise the knowledge gained might well be useless information, which unfortunately has been evident in the past. A critical part of the matrix is that of planning the subject balance and ensuring the topic fulfils the requirements discussed earlier in this chapter.

Balancing the books

In summary, it is appropriate to list the characteristics of balancing the curriculum in diagrammatic form for easy recall. This can be set out as follows:

B readth
A ims and objectives
L earning experiences
A ccount of the
N eeds of
C hildren
E valuating the outcomes

Breadth covers the nine areas of learning and experience already discussed. In relation to the balance it is matched with the curriculum allocation, this being the opportunity provided by teachers for children to experience different curriculum areas. This allocation is linked directly to pupil involvement and what children actually choose to make of the opportunities on offer. It might be better to judge the effectiveness of balance by considering what children actually do rather than what teachers expect them to do. The curriculum is the other means by which we can achieve our stated aims and objectives.

Our aims and objectives are crucial. The aims represent the ideals upon which teachers plan a balanced curriculum and clearly identified objectives are the stepping stones towards the realisation of those aims. There was a time when some educationalists felt it sufficient to provide children with a rich supply of potential learning experiences and thought that, if the classroom presented a sufficiently stimulating environment, effective learning would follow automatically.

It would be ridiculous to deny the value of an attractive and exciting learning environment, but the role of the teacher as an 'enabler' goes beyond that. In planning learning experiences which take account of all the children, attention to balance in respect of class organisation and curriculum planning is of the utmost importance.

Many primary classes today contain children of more than one age group. The HMI 5–9 survey (DES, 1982a) clearly pointed out the value of variety of organisation within individual classes:

> the balance achieved between individual, group and class teaching was particularly important in those classes which contained children of more than one age group. The teachers who used individual and small group teaching approaches in mixed age classes were more effective in establishing the confidence of the children and raising standards of work

Unfortunately, all too often we see children being given learning tasks which do not relate in practical terms to anything they understand or have experienced. Relevance is a key characteristic within the learning process and children need to acquire a particular skill which they can apply to a real situation. It may be necessary to consolidate the learning process by reinforcing the practice through a number of examples, but the children will understand and appreciate what they are doing if they can see the relationship between what they are being required to learn and reality.

There are many teachers who are failing their children in this respect and mathematics is probably the area of the curriculum where the balance has not been achieved as well as it might have been. The 5–9 survey, for example, highlighted the imbalance between the acquisition and use of computational skills:

> In a fifth of the schools there was, throughout, a good balance between learning how to perform a calculation and using it in a practical setting, either within Mathematics or elsewhere in the curriculum. In the remaining four-fifths a good balance was not achieved, and skills were practised in isolation: the work was usually based on self-contained

commercially produced schemes or on graded work cards made in school. Computation often formed the main element in the work, in some schools the sole aim was for the children to reach a standard of efficiency in abstract calculations, though even in these an element of practical work was occasionally included. There was also evidence that children were required to use abstract ideas without the practical experience necessary to a working understanding of them. Younger children were as likely to practise mathematical skills in isolation as were the older childen.

Is this really good enough? The 5–9 survey was published in the same year as the Cockcroft Report (DES, 1982b) and there is evidence of more attention being given now to appropriate balance in the learning activities for young children, particularly in the field of mathematics. The consideration of balance is, however, by no means universal amongst teachers, and in some schools the issue has never been addressed.

Evaluation of the curriculum planning, its delivery and the learning outcomes for children must play an important part in the future education of young children. All children have the right of access to a broad-based and balanced curriculum. Those of us who earn our living within the education service all have a responsibility to see that the teachers, who are the people with front-line responsibility in this respect, have the appropriate initial training and opportunity for further professional development. Within this provision, they must be made aware of the learning needs of children and must be led to a position where they have acquired the skills to become 'enablers' in order to meet these needs. This does not happen overnight and the professional development of teachers is a career-long process.

Just as the juggler perfects his stagecraft in spinning many plates through years of practice and development of his skill, the good teacher will gain more and more insight into pupil needs and will keep more and more plates spinning in the hope that balance and variety will breathe life into the curriculum, thus promoting real and meaningful learning opportunities for the children.

References

DES 1978 *Primary Education in England: a Survey by HM Inspectors of Schools*. HMSO

DES 1982a *Education 5 to 9: an Illustrative Survey of 80 First Schools in England*. HMSO

DES 1982b *Mathematics Counts: Report of the Committee of Inquiry into the Teaching of Mathematics under the Chairmanship of Dr W H Cockcroft*. HMSO

5   Managing individual needs within the classroom

Iain Smithers

Any profession that deals with the human condition should try to remain in awe of that condition, and to remember that it is unique to our planet. As a species we are groups of individuals in multiform social groupings in a constant state of evolutionary change. As teachers we are invited (privileged) to be part of that constant change in a constructive and active role.

I do not believe that there are many answers in education. The dynamics of our society rather ensure that solutions today are problems tomorrow. But we can share our ideas and perceptions of some of these problems and in so doing form new approaches to learning and teaching.

In this discussion I shall look at our subject under the following headings:

1. The individuality of children within the classroom

2. Pressures on the teacher

3. Learning and teaching within effective support conditions

4. Structuring and planning for learning.

The individuality of children within the classroom

Let's start with a question.

Do you as a teacher find yourself pressured into seeing your class as a homogeneous group or as a group of individuals?

Roget's Thesaurus is 'a collection of words and phrases arranged according to ideas rather than alphabetically'. Under 'individual' the following ideas are listed:

unrelated	special
non-uniform	unit
original	one
self	person

I do not think we would argue the point that any class we teach contains on average twenty-five to thirty of these non-uniform special people who are units of one. I could go on to develop lots of different adjectival phrases from my list above but the point is made. Kirby (1981) states that education for individuals is aimed through sensitive relationships and careful organisation at making the most of individual gifts and human potential. We would not dispute this as one of our ultimate aims.

The Plowden Report (1967) stressed the uniqueness of the individual child and the 'enormously wide variability' in physical and intellectual maturity of children of the same age. It urged that any class, however homogeneous, be treated as a body of children needing individual and different provision.

At this point you might care to reflect on the uniqueness of the children in your care. How do their individual intellectual, emotional and physical developments exhibit themselves?

How might modes of thinking and learning be affected by the particular circumstances of their homes, schools, peer groups and the wider world?

You may be helped in your reflections by considering the following example. A class of twenty-seven 8- and 9-year-olds are watching a television broadcast about a trip to the seaside. If we could get 'inside' the heads of our viewers it would be most illuminating.

As a cognitive response each child sees a different picture because he is relating it to a different schema. The child who has been to Spain on holiday thinks of Majorca, the child who goes to Blackpool thinks of rain! Some of the children who have never been to the seaside see only pictures which they know are related to seasides/holidays/visits.

The emotional responses to the programme also will be varied. The child who lost his pocket money running across the sand on his last visit may have a sense of loss engendered by the film. The child who went on a family holiday may relate the seaside pictures to playing with dad, to spending long hours together when normally dad is working away from home. Without further elaboration we can see that this common stimulus has provoked twenty-eight different reactions, twenty-eight unique responses, because there have been twenty-eight understandings and levels of meaningfulness placed on it. What then was the learning in all of this?

Cognitively we can assume that the pupils have learned that seasides contain seascapes and beaches of one sort or another, they don't all look like Blackpool or Majorca and they may be places that have yet to be visited.

Emotional or affective domain learning is harder to assess but we might assume feelings of longing are produced in those with pleasant experiences and perhaps feelings of no more than recognition by those yet to travel. Here, too, there may be mismatch between teacher assumptions and pupil responses.

How can teachers increase their awareness of such individual responses?

How will they design tasks to take account of all these varying responses?

How will they create a sympathetic supportive environment in which their children will grow?

The task is certainly a demanding one: the teachers' success rate will be determined by their ability to balance the needs of their children against the constraints and pressures of their situation.

Pressures on the teacher

As teachers we are perpetually balancing our perceptions of the learning needs of pupils against the expectations of parents, management and society at large.

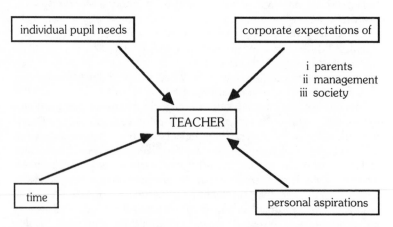

Teachers must constantly be aware of the expectations of the parents of those in their class. Can they satisfy them? How sympathetic are they to the parents' aims and to what degree do they feel constrained by them? (This is most evident in the clash between the three Rs and the so-called 'child centred' approaches.)

Into this picture we must add the expectations of both school management and LEAs/HMIs. Often class teachers feel that more and more is demanded of them in terms of curricular width without anything ever being taken away. Examples of this include craft, design and technology, and microcomputers. A burgeoning timetable will place content and skill pressures on the teachers and in turn on the pupils.

And what of self? We may accept the philosophy put forward by Plowden and Kirby, but how do we feel about ourselves? If we are continually making compromises in time allocation, in objectives set for learners, in management of learning techniques, are we not likely to compromise our own standards? (In the writer's case this was so.)

How are we to resolve the conflict between individual pupil needs and these management pressures?

Learning and teaching within effective support conditions

Elliot-Kemp (1982) is quite categorical that effective teaching can only take place when there is a harmony or congruence within the whole school system. This congruence refers to the total syllabus, the total curriculum, in which teachers' individual contributions to the learning process are ideally in harmony with each other.

To achieve this harmony, or rather to continue to work towards it, must be a high priority task for the new teacher and must be for the more established teacher an embedded skill.

How then are we to achieve this?

Only by accepting that our work is but a contributory part of the child's developing learning continuum.

There must be a willingness on the part of each teacher in the school to be aware of their part in collective policy making. There must be an involvement with the development of through-school policy making. As Elliot-Kemp puts it 'Professional autonomy is thus seen as negotiated within the professional work group or community, and all teachers, it is argued, should be prepared for participation in the shaping of policy within their school'.

So to be an effective teacher is to work at an attitude to learning and teaching which places great emphasis on the aims of the integrated teacher in the integrated system. It is to be part of an effective team.

Where teachers before saw autonomy and a certain geographical isolation, there now must be a willingness to see their contribution as part of a collective or holistic approach. Goals are formed by the staff collectively. Teachers become aware of the need to discuss and share their work with their colleagues, to support others' need for self-development. The emphasis turns to teamwork, coordination and support. We think of the whole school team rather than of the individual teacher.

The conflict referred to earlier is insoluble for the individual teacher in isolation but in the team situation there can be considerable success.

Achieving this success inevitably makes demands on the teacher in terms of knowledge and skills. Elliot-Kemp summarises these as follows:

Knowledge

- self-awareness, helped by feedback from colleagues;
- knowledge of the dynamics of the face-to-face group;
- knowledge of the skills of communicating and relating to others;
- an understanding of the school as a social system;
- the dynamics of change in social systems;
- the state of the art in curriculum development;
- evaluation of self, others, goals, programmes, policies;
- theories of counselling and consulting.

Skills

Pertaining to task achievement
- initiating of ideas and activities;
- information seeking and dissemination;
- elaborating alternative possibilities for action and their linked consequences;
- coordinating ideas, plans or people;
- challenging and evaluating facts, opinions, procedures, practicality or logic;
- responding positively to confrontation and challenge from others;
- classifying and recording data;
- allocating resources;
- attending and listening (a vital yet neglected skill area).

Pertaining to building and maintenance of relationships
- resolving conflicts and mediating differences;
- facilitating the participation of others;
- regulating communication flow in group interaction;
- appropriate self-disclosure;

- communicating warmth, respect and support;
- communicating accurate empathic understanding;
- helping and consulting others;
- collaborating with others;
- sharing ideas, resources, problems, goals;
- demonstrating team member identity in addition to individual identity.

To sum up, the conditions for effective learning and teaching are:

1. integrated collaborative systems in schools that value the teacher and child;
2. systems of overt care for both teachers and learners.

It follows that:

1. meeting these conditions must be a long-term aim and activity of the school team; and
2. these conditions will be most effectively met when there is a shared view of learning as a collaborative venture between teacher and child.

Learning, a collaborative venture

Collaborative teachers give time and support to the learner, listen to him as he works through the task, give guidance when he has problems, initiate remediation and diagnose the needs of the learner in action to ensure a task match.

They identify and value the learning processes that the child uses instead of simply evaluating or assessing the outcomes.

Reflect on this point.

Often work with children is justified by the amount that they cover as evidenced by filled jotters and covered walls. Perhaps we need to value more the *ways* in which they work, viz., by talking with them about their task, by recording discussions on tape and by valuing the written planning that they do when starting a task.

Collaborative teachers believe that when children are at the receiving end of instructions the skills of task management are low. When they allow the pupil to suggest learning strategies and potential learning outcomes, then the child's skills are brought forward through a successful task match.

For example, the child who writes out a plan of a piece of written work and discusses this plan with his teacher in a writers' conference is both learning new skills and evidencing his work.

Consider too our conditions for effective learning and teaching for pupil and teacher. Will the pupil's self-image not be enhanced by the respect which the teacher shows for his efforts, and through the partnership between learner and teacher which he sees existing to help him? Teachers will feel supported in their critical use of time by a support system within the whole school management that values their care for the pupil's self-image and their utilisation of that time.

Children feel good about themselves when we as teachers feel good about ourselves. When we feel that we are doing a good job, valued within our community, valuing others and supporting them, then we can pass on that model/message to our learners.

Teachers in developing this collaborative approach to learning and teaching are prepared to allow pupils to initiate new ideas, to face problems and formulate approaches, and to discuss outcomes to develop new approaches in a variety of media. *As a result of their success the learners become increasingly independent of the teachers.*

Structuring and planning for learning

My belief is that effective learning and teaching takes place when we match appropriate tasks to the needs of pupils.

Desforges (1976) identifies four main types of task:

> incremental
> restructuring
> enrichment
> practice.

Incremental tasks introduce new ideas or skills; restructuring demands the invention or discovery of an idea; enrichment demands the application of familiar skills to new problems and practice demands the timing of new skills on familiar problems.

The teachers identify which task is to be matched to which child in the light of their summative assessment of the child's current development arising from earlier collaborative learning.

How does this operate in practice?

I want to make an assumption that for most of us learning and teaching in the primary school is structured by using a centre of interest or theme as the vehicle for our planning. For some there will always be room for the child to negotiate certain aspects of study which interests him at specific times. For others the learner's autonomy may be such that teachers will follow the natural learning of the child (Rowland, 1984).

I believe that in planning for the individual, and to exist within the pressure model, we must be free to group the individual in different types of group according to the task, sometimes in groups of children with similar task abilities and sometimes within groups who have a common task outcome (Kirby, 1981). Whichever is the case, the planning should follow a similar pattern.

Planning for learning and teaching

1. *Analyse* pupil work to establish current attainment levels in the various skill areas and current experience of key ideas.
2. *Identify* from this analysis the skills and key ideas to be developed, consolidated or introduced.
3. *Select* topic and brainstorm for sub-themes and content.
4. *Match* sub-themes with skills and key ideas identified in 2. above. Decision: Will topic selected support identified learning?
   Yes   No
5. *Consider* and note resources needed for work.
6. *Plan* first sub-theme in detail.
7. *Initiate* the work with children.
8. *Assess* the pupil learning and match against 2. Evaluate and . . .

Let's move through this process step by step.

1. *Analysis*   If we assume that the theme of work is to be multidisciplinary, we must establish which skills and key ideas we are to elicit, e.g. will our theme develop language skills and/or the ideas associated with historical research and reconstruction? Will our theme concentrate on geographical skills and/or explore man's interaction with his environment?

In approaching this I can suggest nothing that is unique or new to you. We can identify with and share in our pupils' aspirations by adopting the collaborative approach; by getting 'close' to our pupils and talking with them; by forming discussion groups with our writers about their intentions and techniques as well as their outcomes; by asking them to help plan out a particular problem to be solved in science or mathematics; by observing how children approach a task, which strategies they adopt, which medium they choose to record ideas and feelings, we can identify and share in their aspirations, strengths and weaknesses.

In short, I suggest that this analysis of children learning becomes a profile which will serve to record successes, failures and stages in learning and which will assist in matching tasks to observed needs.

I hope it is clear that I am not suggesting that you do all of this right away with each child! Don't forget you are part of the integrated collaborative system discussed earlier. I am attempting to outline a realistic structure for you which will allow you both to build up a picture of your learners as individuals and also to profile their learning activities and achievements.

2. *Identification*   As the pupil profiles are developed, your general overview of the curriculum needs of your class will suggest areas/themes for development. These become the vehicle for learning. I want to suggest to you that it is as important to allow for consolidation of learned skills as it is to allow for the introduction of new ones. Children must feel that they have purpose in their learning; thus the individual who finds recording by graphic representation easier than writing must be given opportunity to use this skill successfully. An enhanced self-image through success will always lead to more success, I believe.

3. *Selection and brainstorm*   This is the easiest part for most of us. Having analysed our children's needs and identified the tasks relevant to those needs we should select a topic or theme to be our vehicle for learning.

Most schools will have a policy document with a topic grid but care should be taken to ensure that the topic chosen will support the learning identified.

4. *Matching*   This stage is an interesting one, I think. We have taken our topic or centre of interest and broken it down into sub-themes and now we need to match the identified skills and key ideas to these sub-themes.

Let me give you an example:

TOPIC:	**Communication**
SUB-THEME	**Newspapers**
SKILLS TO BE DEVELOPED:	**Note taking** **Finding the main idea** **Sequencing** **Report writing**

PLAN OF WORK: **Through the production of a class newspaper certain children will be using note-taking skills and will be introduced to report writing as a development. Other children will be using news articles to practice finding the main idea, and so on.**

In other words, within each sub-theme tasks will be matched to individual children to develop skills identified by the teacher through analysis and profiling.

Steps 5, 6 and 7 are fairly straightforward and do not need developing here.

8. *Assessment*   Let me ask you some questions.

What problems, if any, do you have with assessment and record keeping? What would you like your system to do for you? How time consuming is this?

I believe I offered you part of a solution to this when I described my view of analysis and profiling. As you identify individual pupil needs and match them to planned work, their outcomes will represent statements of current attainment.

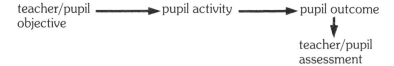

In this final stage, I feel it necessary to invite the learner to form his own assessment of his outcomes. Sometimes this is a simple process of self-marking, but often it will be a rather more articulated assessment based upon his own evaluation of his work. This is perhaps particularly evident in the early years of education where the learner has an expectation that he will be asked by the teacher about his opinion of his work.

In discussion of the task set, the pupil will have outlined the outcomes as he sees them. At a simple level this may well be no more than the successful writing down of a mathematical computation or perhaps the completion of a mapping exercise.

At a more complex level, the learner may be asked for his opinion of his performance in a group problem solving activity. As Rowland

(1984) puts it, we must seek a critical relationship in which we, pupil and teacher, come to know what we are thinking about and aiming for.

For realistic tasks to be set from this assessment teachers need to know not just what they are aiming for but also what their colleagues as a whole are aiming for. They need to know that their efforts with their groups of individuals are part of a progression which has been designed by a team.

What form will this profile take?

I'm not sure that this is for me to say. Space, resources and your own inventiveness will decide that, but one suggestion I have for you is to provide some form of plastic wallet or file for each child. This might be used to hold samples of rough plans, early attempts at story writing and paintings in various media; and by you, the teacher, some diary jottings about discussions you have had in planning groups, observations of the individual in free/directed activity and in interacting with others, etc.

Summary

In this chapter we have considered the uniqueness of each child – a uniqueness born out of environmental factors outside teachers' control but nevertheless meriting careful consideration in their provision for individual needs.

The constraints of the school situation, parental and community expectations and teachers' own aspirations create a pressure that can be insuperable for the individual. I have suggested, therefore, that effective teaching will arise from a collaborative support system which actively involves all members of staff in a working definition of the school policy and practice.

I have further suggested that effective learning by children occurs when teacher and child collaborate in the planning, execution and assessment of the learning task. Selection of the learning task is not random but the result of careful analysis by the teacher of individual attitudes, attainments and aspirations.

I wish you success in your approaches to learning and teaching.

References

DES 1967 *Children and their Primary Schools* (The Plowden Report). HMSO

Desforges C 1985 Matching tasks to children. In Bennett N, Desforges C (eds) *Recent Advances in Classroom Research*. Scottish Academic Press

Elliot-Kemp J, Rogers C 1982 *The Effective Teacher: A Person-Centred Development Guide*. Pavic Publications

Kirby N 1981 *Personal Values in Education*. Harper & Row

Rowland S 1984 *The Enquiring Classroom*. Falmer Press

6 Arranging the classroom environment

Clive Wilkinson

'*Accessibility to learning opportunities is the keynote to the way in which the environment is arranged*'.

Alice Yardley, The Organisation of the Infant School

Many teachers spend hours in planning in great detail aspects of learning for children. They consider factors of time, depth, differentiation, resources available, the needs of individuals and much more; the list seems never ending. However one item often overlooked in much of this detailed planning is the organisation of the environment in which the learning will take place.

It often needs a change of classroom or a move of school to make many teachers look at the way in which their classroom is arranged. Even then, the beginning of year 'move round' of furniture is not necessarily done with regard to curriculum planning but is often a case of how best to arrange the room to avoid damage to the teachers' limbs. Very often teachers inherit items of furniture which they never use and which, as they would realise if they thought long and hard, they don't really want. Such items usually become the collecting place for anything that does not have a 'natural' home: the unfinished model, the paintings that need mounting, the pile of magazines and newspapers that you know will be useful some day, the box of computer printout paper a friendly parent has given, etc. This is not to say that classrooms don't need or shouldn't have such items, more a case of raising the question of where you keep them.

All too often an intended 'nature table' gets buried under a sea of unfinished work and other artefacts which 'will come in useful sometime'. The teacher's desk can also become a 'problem area', in so much as if often suffers from the answer to the child's question, 'Where shall I put this?' To that the teacher's reply is often, 'Oh, put it on my desk.'

Children and teachers work in many types of 'space', from classroom to open-plan area. Whatever the environment, it is important to ask the following questions: What do we expect the children to do in the 'learning environment'? How will we expect them to do it? The resulting room layout will also reflect the personality and philosophical ideals of the organising teacher, be it the classic 'four rows in front of the blackboard' or a far more informal arrangement of furniture.

If one of our strategies as teachers is to provide for children to become independent learners, then we may need to consider some of the following.

Zones of activity – What are the children doing in each part of the classroom?

Loads – How many children will work in each zone? A wet, messy area, overloaded with children, may cause trouble.

Pathways – Is there a stream of traffic through zones? Can this traffic be minimised by a change in classroom layout?

Resources – Are the appropriate resources based in each zone, so that children are involved in the least amount of movement?

Supervision – Can the teacher supervise from all points in the area?

Peripheral planning – How can the teacher use the edges of the room?

Display – How is it presented and what are its uses and functions?

Ideally, any class area needs to be as flexible as humanly possible, simultaneously providing security for the children who work there and acting as a stimulating environment to all. The words 'stimulating environment' roll easily off the tongue, yet which particular features make it such? What is it that draws us from the classroom door and makes us want to explore? What creates excitement for the children? What is that special something that distinguishes some class areas in the school from others?

We are assured of the certainty that there is no magic answer, no correct formula, no 'ideal' room layout. Many children are taught in classrooms where the display boards are too high, the radiators are in the wrong places, the sink is badly placed or absent altogether, the windows are too high or too low, the furniture is too old or the wrong height, the room lacks storage, doors that should open in open out and, almost inevitably, there is never enough SPACE. However, little of this will change, and no progress will be made if we merely continue to cry, 'if only I had better resources, if only I had more space, if only I had better children', etc., etc.

⊻ Teaching should be about the positive and about making the best use of what we have. So, whilst we remember that many aspects of the learning environment are inadequate, let's start from the positive and think of ways in which our areas can be made more stimulating, productive and inviting.

It is hoped that many activities in the primary class area are practical, active and derived from first-hand experience. In any practical situation there are implications of space, resources and how children learn. You will know, of course, that to have everybody in the class simultaneously involved in exactly the same practical activity is not always making the best use of space, resources or teacher time. Many practical activities have been cursed by teachers because the classroom has appeared chaotic when thirty children have all been involved. Such scenarios are common.

Space planning

The success or failure of the room as a working environment depends much upon the thought given in its planning, and fundamental to this planning is the division between 'messy' and 'clean' areas, and between 'noisy' and 'quiet' areas. It is essential that one type of activity can take place in a constructive and mostly uninhibited way without disturbing the concentration needed for another. In the process of planning, it is necessary for the teacher to ask questions such as the following.

Are there any areas of the room which are underused, and therefore is the present arrangement the best use of space?

What appears to be the best use of space sometimes permits the room to have vastly underused areas, owing to the mismanagement of time. For example, if a book corner has been established but children are only permitted to use it during the last thirty minutes of the day, or if an art area has been designated and is infrequently used during the week, then careful space planning is pointless. Clearly then, the use of space can be seen to be closely connected with the teacher's and children's use of time. Perhaps the message is, do not establish 'areas' unless you are intending to make effective use of them.

Are the resources or children's trays so grouped that they create congestion at the beginning of every work session? Is it possible to re-locate the equipment to allow the children to make better use of it?

Does the room always look untidy and cluttered even when it has just been tidied? What then makes the room seem so crowded? Are there unnecessary or infrequently used items which would be better placed in a store elsewhere in the school? In addition to encouraging tidiness in the children, it is important for the teacher systematically and objectively to scrutinise the room and ask which items are permanently needed for the smooth running of the room, which need re-location and which need labelling so that tidiness can be maintained. Indeed, is the teacher's desk merely a surface which attracts clutter, and to which children gather? Could it be dispensed with altogether and a more productive item or space be substituted? It is advisable to ask a colleague to help with any clearing-up operation, and talk through ideas and practical solutions to problems. There is a phrase in gardening that your worst enemy should prune your roses; perhaps this is true also of classroom clear-ups. The squirrel-like nature of most teachers means that they are reluctant to throw anything away. Stories of teachers who have been in the same classroom for decades are legion, and provide amusing staffroom anecdotes.

Have all possibilities of using areas adjacent to the classroom been exhausted? Corridors, parts of cloakrooms, outdoor covered areas, etc. can provide ideal working conditions for certain activities.

The class area must be functional and lead to the formation of good working habits. It must be easily supervised, so that whilst being unobstructive, the teacher can maintain an overview of the room. Room planning must provide free access to the teacher wherever she is, and also ease of access to resources without overcrowding or requiring seated children to move unnecessarily. It must also provide ease of access to the child's own property, to display areas and to all room exits. In the planning consideration must have been given to how the children will be grouped and, if learning bays exist, how they will be arranged.

Learning bays are useful as they allow for the appropriate equipment to be stored near to the activity taking place and hence reduce the amount of movement around the room. They also facilitate groups of children working together on a similar subject. Teachers should be aware of the importance of using the periphery of the room as children's work space. Observing many classrooms, it is noticeable that usually children are seated centrally and benches and tables are used for storage and display rather than for children to

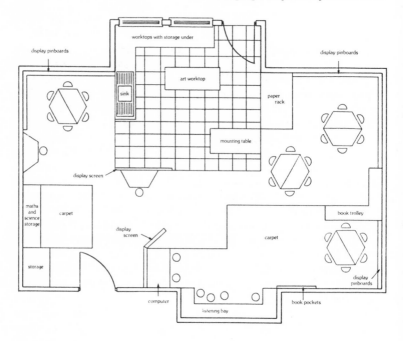

Figure 6.1 – Classroom plan

Here is an example of a classroom layout showing a teacher's thinking as to where items of furniture should be placed in accordance with learning activities planned.

Questions still to be addressed include
- Where would children's storage units be best placed?
- Would easy chairs/cushions provide a better reading environment?
- Does this plan fulfil the criteria expressed at the beginning of the chapter, including *zones of activity, loads, pathways,* etc.?

work at. It is possible that certain badly organised classrooms, when the territory occupied by the teacher's desk and the underused areas of the room, such as the edges, are taken into account, children may be working in only 60 per cent of the available space. Learning bays permit the maximum use of the outside edges of the room.

Learning bays are usually created by setting cupboards at right angles to the wall, or by using screens, open shelves and tables. Open shelves are particularly useful as they fulfil the dual functions of dividing and providing a storage point. Dividers should not be so placed as to make the children feel cut off from the rest of the group or from the teacher. Low screens, or corrugated card set on tables at the shoulder height of the teacher, provide useful vertical display space and also allow the teacher to maintain an overview of the children's activities.

It is likely that the size of learning bays will change frequently, according to the nature of the work and the groupings of children. Mobility of dividing material is therefore essential. Cupboards on castors, supported corrugated card and light, purpose built, double-sided screens are useful, whereas shelf units and heavy wooden screens require a more permanent site. The arrangement of tables can create small bays. Trapezoidal tables provide great variation in layout, and higher 'standing work' tables are also useful. Indeed, if the children are provided with worktops at a standing level, it is possible to reduce the amount of space required for chairs. Is there a need for all the children to be seated on chairs at all times during the day?

When planning a room, it is not always advisable to launch straight into the movement of heavy and awkward furniture. As Brown and Precious (1968) suggest:

> It is a good idea to draw the room to scale on graph paper. Each piece of furniture can then be drawn to scale and cut out so that it is possible to arrange the activity or subject areas in miniature and easily find what seems to be the most advantageous arrangement.

Storage

The efficiency of storage systems within the area greatly affects the success of the working environment. They need to look tidy and to be large enough to contain everything they are supposed to hold. They must use space as wisely and economically as possible. All spaces contained within them must be clearly labelled to facilitate ease of resource location and return, and they must contain all items required for the job the child has to do. If the storage unit must have doors or screens, then sliding doors or curtains are preferable to hinged doors. If there are hinged doors fitted, remove them altogether to save space. Wall-mounted card pockets and small tubs provide good storage and need little space. Tall wooden cupboards, only the lower shelves of which are suitable for children, may be turned on their sides and converted into long, low units. They then also provide a low top surface for three-dimensional display.

It is possible to convert many old and apparently obsolete items of school furniture to enhance the classroom environment and relieve storage problems.

Room dividers – Use can be made of: custom-made screens, garden trellis, garden netting, drapes, corrugated card, clothes horses with drapes and children's coat racks. A double locker desk can be converted by fixing lengths of 6 ft (2 in × 1 in) batoning to the legs and back of the desk, on to which pinboard is secured.

Useful ideas for – Double locker desks back to back, covered with
conversion   chipboard or plywood to make a table top.
Chipboard and batoning to make benches.
Stage blocks for use as mini-display tables.
Assorted sized cardboard boxes covered with hessian or fabric to act as plinths for display.
Strong, attractively covered boxes, turned on their sides to make storage 'cubby holes'.
Collapsible tables such as decorators' pasting tables or trestle tables for display.
Large coffee tins covered with sticky-backed plastic for use as storage containers for rulers, paintbrushes, etc.
Garden seed trays for storage of all kinds.
Bricks, breeze blocks and planks for book shelving.
Washing lines suspended across the room, from which to hang mobiles, displays, etc.

Display

It can be said that the aims and purposes of display are:

1. To stimulate interest in a given topic.
2. To present information in a clear and concise way, communicating to those involved and not involved in the work.
3. To encourage children in their work, and instil a sense of pride and value in each contribution, also helping children to develop a critical appraisal of their working space.

How then can this be achieved when children are daily subjected to such a variety of visual stimuli?

Firstly, the way in which the display is arranged can either give a cluttered 'fussy' impression or can be visually attractive and create interest and stimulation. Although it is sometimes important to create the display instantly, as children finish work, unless some thought is given to the finished result a rather *ad hoc* display often results. To have planned the varying sizes of the paper and an approximate layout beforehand is preferable, and to collect together groups of items before arranging them also helps.

How then are groupings formed? Perhaps according to size; or by collecting up work by a particular child; or compiling a set of a written piece, a picture and a computer printout on a similar theme. There are infinite layouts to be chosen, but thought should be given to whether the display is purely for visual impact, to communicate information or to make use of tactile stimuli. Lettering, so often used at the top of the display, would perhaps have more impact if it were sometimes placed centrally, or offset to one side and at a lower level. Letter templates, although not exclusively suitable, save time, are visually pleasing and can be used by the children. They can draw round them and cut out along their lines, thus involving them more in the construction of the display. Freehand lettering by the teacher, unless she has a particular talent in this direction, can be time-consuming and poor. Good cut-out lettering is often spoiled by using a staple gun to attach the letters; glue or spray mount is infinitely preferable. Also worthy of consideration is whether lettering is superfluous to the display. A good display sometimes communicates by itself.

Some examples of possible layouts are shown in Figures 6.2 and 6.3. You will notice that they are organised and uncluttered and take account of the shape and size of a piece of work and the 'symmetry' of the overall display. It is important to take the size of the display board into account; a sea of small items randomly and widely spaced on a large board can look insignificant and lost. Also, teachers often 'trim down' the work to fit the space, without having regard for the balance intended by the child.

To give added interest, it is also important to use a variety of shapes for display, rather than relying on the standard rectangle, although to mix shapes within a display can give a rather messy look. It is useful to remember that displays should always have a common theme, be it shape, colour, size or texture, etc. and that only one variable need be included, i.e. let the shape remain the same whilst the size is variable, or let the colour remain the same while the texture is variable. Try to establish a focal point, or points, within the display, and radiate from them, allowing the eye to concentrate and understand, and not wander around searching for a point of interest. Flat wall displays can be given added interest with the use of slight relief, such as paper sculpture and quilling.

The use of colour is crucial. All too often, pictures are mounted on black sugar paper and added to a single backing colour, which is frequently determined by the remaining choice on the paper rack. Subtle use of colour adds a great deal to a display and encourages visual discrimination by the children. The bright, garish stimuli of

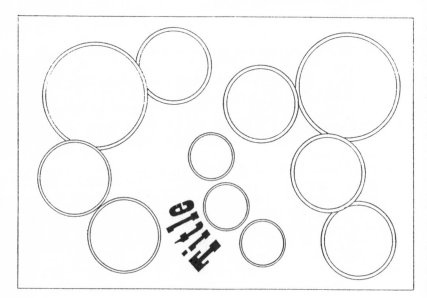

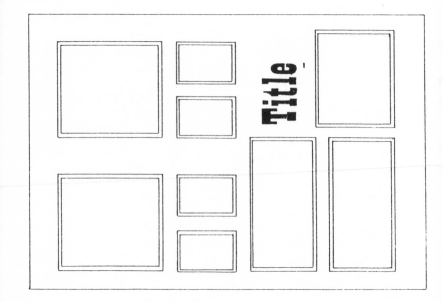

Figure 6.2

Figure 6.3

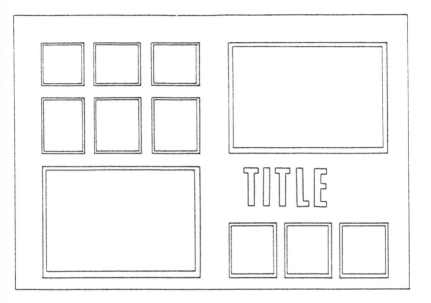

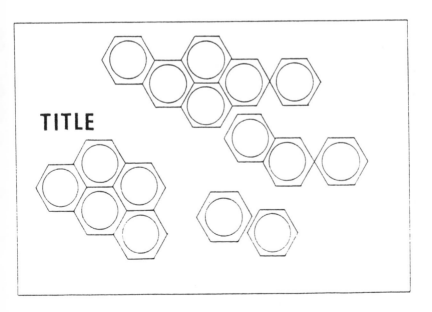

television, advertising and comics perhaps require balancing by subtle, quiet and neutral tones in the class area. Some ideas are shown in Figure 6.4, showing degree of tone and never using more than three variations. The choice of one colour, using a light and dark variation, is effective, especially when combined with a new texture, e.g. a shiny paper in the same colour. A background colour is intended to complement and enhance the display, rather than to overpower it or compete with it.

Many displays give thought to colour and yet pay little attention to variations in texture. As a backing, fabrics, corrugated card, hessian, felt, wallpaper, polystyrene, rush matting, carpet squares, painted peg board and shiny paper provide interesting surfaces. They can be laid flat or folded, gathered, ridged and hung to enhance the overall effect. They are particularly useful in the creation of a corner display, to create the illusion of mystique, especially when used in combination with discreet lighting. Corrugated card has a multitude of uses: as free standing display; as islands, set upon low worktop surfaces, supported with tables and chairs, etc. Natural objects, such as bark, stones and shells and man-made objects such as pottery, woodwork and metalwork are useful in such a display but, again, attention must be paid to their size as many small isolated objects separate from one another simply look messy. The tendency is to move heaven and earth to force the children to make their work unnaturally large. Big is often beautiful, but small also has its place.

It is important to consider whether the objects on display are to be handled or merely viewed, as this will affect their arrangement. If it is to be the former, then clear, non-movable labelling, perhaps stapled on to the backing cloth, is advisable, so that the children know exactly where each item should be returned to. Labels should be clear and uniform in size and not appear as if added as an afterthought. Also included, if appropriate, should be viewing aids, such as microscopes and magnifying glasses. Displays with many three-dimensional items should give consideration to height. Rather than place each object upon one horizontal surface, perhaps use a cardboard block, or a piece of staging covered with a suitable drape to give height to the objects at the back or in the centre, or to give a side focus.

Children's work invariably looks its best when mounted. However, that is not to say that the teacher must spend laborious hours at this task. Children should not regard their contribution towards the display as being finished when they hand their piece of paper over to the teacher. The skills learned through mounting their own work are most valuable. How to use the paper trimmer, judging the right size of the border – and reducing it when they realise that small borders look better than large ones, understanding the use of

Figure 6.4

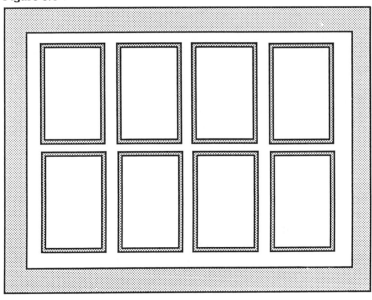

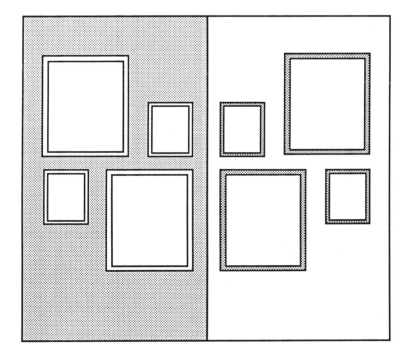

colour and how to organise 'their' display, all allow them to feel more responsible for the working environment. To facilitate this, a 'display preparation area' within the classroom is most useful. A table permanently housing the paper cutter, a wastepaper bin underneath, scissors, glue and an adjacent paper rack, saves time and effort that would be needed to collect these items together each time. If children are to help themselves to the agreed mounting paper, then it must be accessible; deep shelving prevents the children from obtaining the paper underneath. If possible, one or two shades of colour only should occupy one shelf, and so the more shelves the better.

It is essential to include a variety of displays in order to try to fulfil as many aims as possible. Fixed or semi-permanent displays of vases, plants, etc.; a picture gallery display; a work stimulating display which includes instructions and work ideas; a viewing display containing items of written, pictorial and three-dimensional work by the children; and an 'instant' constantly changing display of items brought in by the children each morning, and which are of particular interest, might be a valuable combination within the work area. Children's standards are set by what is offered to them, and displays should therefore be of the highest quality. This should not mean, however, that displays are the artwork of the teacher, filled in by the children. If we do not trust the children, and insist that a template is frequently used, they will believe that they cannot do well enough with their own freehand efforts. Although their first few efforts at arranging and organising displays may be rather ragged, precision is not learned by the teacher taking the task away from them. A combination of teacher directed and organised displays together with those of the children maintains the balance. It is important to look at displays in other schools as a form of inspiration, although to imitate is a mistake, as a stimulating, relevant and aesthetic display in one school can look sadly out of place and character in another.

It may be said then, that the appearance of a room needs to look attractive, interesting and stimulating, although as Brown and Precious (1968) point out, it is essentially a workshop for children and if it is well used should appear as such. However, a well-organised and thoroughly planned working environment will not only fulfil all its requirements but inevitably ensure a settled, secure and well-behaved group of children. This organisation should be the result of a planned curriculum. We should never arrive at a situation whereby we are inventing activities to fit our organisation. As the classroom evolves, the teacher must always be forward looking and thoughtful towards change, not only in formulating ideas but in implementing them. Remember that many good ideas falter on the rocks of implementation. Above all, the most apparently

Figure 6.5 – Questions to ask yourself when organising the classroom environment

1. Have you gathered a sufficient range of resources and organised your space
   - for the spread of ability in your class
   - for the difference in learning styles
   - to provide a wide choice of teaching methods
   - to enable children to follow a wide range of interests
   - to provide for the range of activities for which you have planned, incorporating study, workshop and library facilities?

2. Are there resources for
   - the slow learner
   - children with specific learning difficulties
   - children with behavioural/emotional problems?

3. Are the equipment and resources you use (especially books) of a standard of quality in content and attractiveness to convey the message to the learner that you consider 'only the best is good enough for our children'?

   Have you examined your stock of resources to see if the books convey any hidden messages about sex roles, race and class?

   Are your reference books up-to-date?

4. Have you considered the following in relation to display
   - setting aside a regular time to devote to displaying work
   - increasing your knowledge of materials available by consulting catalogues and consortium lists
   - providing yourself with the basic tools?

   Basic tools for display:

   Rotatrim cutter
   cutting knife
   steel rule
   range of adhesives
   pinpush
   sewing pins
   pliers
   staple gun
   stapler
   staple remover – lever type
   hook pins for drapes
   range of pens
   large scissors
   blu-tak
   letter templates
   drawing pins for use in preliminary arrangement of display
   cutting board

insurmountable practical classroom problems can be tackled successfully purely by the inventiveness of the teacher, especially when working with colleagues and respecting their views and advice. For the most part, classrooms work well when there is a sense of rigour, care and obvious organisation. This acts as a security for all the partners in education: children, teachers and parents. It is a valuable, non-verbal communication, often underestimated by the teacher.

References

Brown M, Precious N 1968 *The Integrated Day in the Primary School.* Ward Lock Educational
Yardley A 1976 *The Organisation of the Infant School.* Evans

Further reading

Corbin T J 1970 *Display in Schools.* Pergamon Press
Dean J 1983 *Organising Learning in the Primary Classroom.* Croom Helm
Dean J 1972 *Room to Learn; WORKING SPACE.* Evans
Dean J 1973 *Room to Learn; DISPLAY.* Evans
Jarman C 1972 *Display and Presentation in Schools.* A & C Black

7 Making the best use of teacher time

Ray Arnold

The management of teacher time is now very much more of a conscious issue than it was. Time and its use are very much at the forefront of educational debate. The class teacher and the children she teaches are the focus of a whole web of complex, interrelated issues within which the management of time is crucial.

There is no doubt that class teaching is becoming a more complex job and that this is leading to a severe increase in pressure of time on the teacher. Some of the issues which impinge upon her professional life are trivial, infuriating and, sometimes, just plain idiotic, but many are not and are highly important aspects of the education of children. Accountability to parents and the community generally, current research on conditions for effective classroom learning, and current contributions to curriculum debates all have implications for teacher time. There are important new perspectives on equal opportunities and multicultural education which must have the teacher's attention and which have a proper claim on classroom time. There is no way in which these and similar issues can be avoided by the true professional who is seeking to make the best use of her time in the interest of effective learning by the children. She very much feels the pressure of time in trying to provide a broad curriculum, and to do that without communicating an undue sense of haste, indeed making time for those relaxed yet purposeful exchanges which are at the core of good primary practice, requires careful planning. There are, thankfully, only a small minority of teachers who see the school day as an empty void to be filled with disconnected activities, 'fillers', books of exercises and prepackaged lessons.

The purpose of this chapter is to help professionals manage their time more efficiently and to put forward a view, backed by current research, about *how* time should be spent in class. Underpinning much of what I have to say are the findings of the Junior School Project, a research programme undertaken by the Research and Statistics Branch of ILEA, now published (ILEA, 1986). These findings will be discussed in more detail later.

Another underpinning which influences the whole chapter is a broad notion of what constitutes achievement. The idea of achievement having four broad aspects is most eloquently stated in the Hargreaves Report (1984) and they apply equally to children in the primary school. He defines achievement as follows:

1. The capacity to retain factual propositional knowledge and to select and deploy it effectively, especially in written form. This is individual rather than group achievement.
2. The ability to apply knowledge – practical skills, problem solving and the like.
3. Personal and social skills – cooperation, relationships, initiative, working in groups successfully.
4. Motivation and commitment – perseverence under difficulty, positive acceptance of failure, self-confidence for learning.

It is a matter for concern that so many people regard achievement as belonging only under the first heading and think that the proper purpose of schools is to concentrate only on that aspect. I suggest that teacher time must be spent equally on the other three aspects that the report describes; schools can and do have a strong beneficial influence in helping children to achieve in all four areas, not just the first.

Techniques

There is a problem that we must confront before we can examine time management techniques. It is the very bad connotations which the word 'management' has for many primary teachers. To many, the word smacks of business of commercial attitudes which they feel are ill-suited to the purposes of education. Other vivid images are conjured up involving an uncaring, unfeeling way of working in which only a quantified end product is important, not real people and their emotions. The word is also associated in some colleagues' minds with people who think that all school problems, and educational problems generally, can be solved by a dose of management theory or, more subtly, by the application of efficient management skills.

Theory by itself never solves anything. I do, however, believe that schools would be even happier and more productive places if all the partners in the educational enterprise had more relevant management skills and applied them. In fact the management skills of successful primary practitioners are prodigiously wide-ranging. A colleague of mine recently married a successful businessman who is now very interested in, and supportive of, primary education. He is quite astonished at the extraordinary complexity of classroom life and the sheer range of organizational skills that are necessary to run a successful primary class. The point is that these management skills are not ends in themselves, but are at the service of the children and their education.

Bearing all these points in mind, let us now look at some possible time management techniques for the classroom teacher.

Step 1

It is crucial to appreciate that time is a resource like money and equipment, and it is often in shorter supply than both of these. However, it is a resource with certain characteristics of its own. It has been said by Drucker that 'The supply of time is totally inelastic. Time is totally perishable and cannot be stored. Time is irreplaceable ... there is no substitute for time'.

While (at least in theory!) a school can obtain extra money or equipment, it cannot generally obtain extra time, particularly class contact time with the children. It is important therefore to take care of precious class time and use it properly, in other words, *manage* it. That is not to suggest organizing every second of it, but being aware of time as a scarce resource and to treat it as such.

Step 2

Try calculating roughly how much time you and your class spend together in teaching and learning situations, however widely interpretated. Subtract the time spent 'going to and coming from', playtimes unofficially extended, dealing with unexpected crises and the like. Suddenly time begins to look like a very scarce resource indeed. Hopefully an awareness of this will lead to you take what steps you can to minimize unnecessary loss, although some things you really cannot do anything about.

Step 3

Try and find out how you actually spend time in class, not how you think you do! There are various strategies for doing this. One is to keep a time log over a day or a week, entering at fixed time intervals or during a natural break in the day what had happened in the previous session. Another method is to enter significant events or activities as they happen, together with a note of the time. Both these are difficult to implement in a busy classroom but the results almost provide some remarkable insights in terms of what is actually happening and what you are actually doing. You may find that you are spending a disproportionate amount of time on activities which you would not wish to give a high priority to! One very common finding from such an exercise is that a considerable amount of time is given to classroom routine and its implementation.

Teachers are often horrified when they realise the amount of time they spend on matters like finding pencils and paper, directing children on minor matters which have only a very tenuous link with the classroom learning situation, and also on unnecessary interventions as the children are working. This is, of course, not to say that classroom routine and teacher intervention are unimportant – they are absolutely crucial to successful primary practice. A routine is a means to an end, and it fails in its purpose if it has to be constantly re-established and re-explained. Teacher intervention can be highly significant for learning but it can also be an irrelevant distraction. For those of you interested in finding out more about the 'time log', it is discussed in more detail in Craig (1987).

Step 4

Another revealing exercise is to note briefly, over a day or so, any interruptions to classroom work that you consider unproductive – messages from the headteacher, maybe! Go through this list and see if any of these interruptions can be avoided or dealt with in some other way. It would be helpful if you could find a colleague to discuss your list with, and even better if she has a list herself. Not all unproductive interruptions can be dealt with on one's own, of course, so it may be necessary to raise some of these issues with colleagues and with the headteacher. It is not a bad thing to have the reputation that you and your class do not appreciate being interrupted for trivial reasons, but that you welcome people coming into your class at appropriate times and with appropriate purposes. I know that I am very welcome in all the classes at my school and spend a good deal of time in them, but I try to be sensitive about this point and responsive to colleagues who hint on occasions that this is not the right time for them.

Step 5

One of the greatest aids to efficient time management is having clear priorities. To a great extent, this involves careful long-term classroom planning and organization, and discussion of this lies outside the scope of this chapter. However, a teacher can usefully set herself some limited priorities or objectives on a daily or weekly basis, within the context of her overall curriculum and organizational planning. If done sensibly and flexibly, this can be very helpful for the management of her time. It is probably best done on a daily basis. A rough classification of priorities could be along the lines of:

A   I **MUST** do this today
B   I **SHOULD** do this today
C   I would **LIKE TO** do this today.

These priorities could be personal ones or could relate to things you wish the children to do, but they need to be short-term and specific. Too many of them will be very daunting. The examples below are coded to correspond with the classification given above.

A   Make sure the whole class finish their book reviews
B   Work with a small group of children who are making certain spelling mistakes in common
C   See the head about a class outing
A   Finish a special needs report form
C   Change the display in the book corner
B   Start a group on one of the newly prepared practical mathematics activities

Of course, there will be many other activities in the classroom and much to deflect you from your purpose. It is, however, very satisfying to be able to deal with at least the A-rated matters and hopefully some of the others during a particular day. It is important to feel that you have organized yourself to achieve some of your priorities.

Step 6

It is important when planning your time to make the distinction between what is urgent and what is important. The task which is both urgent and important is much rarer than one might think, and, generally speaking, it is not too difficult to recognize as such. What it is all too easy to do is to inflate the importance of urgent but trivial tasks. So much time and energy can disappear into dealing with immediately pressing matters that there is no time left for longer-term important issues. Of course there must be some crisis management and immediate response to situations, but as much time as possible needs to be directed towards important classroom tasks. Sadly, it tends to be the crises and their various outcomes which remain in the mind at the end of a school day, rather than important but unspectacular achievement and progress. Situations differ so much that it is hard to give specific advice, but to be aware of the distinction is an important step forward in thinking about time allocation.

Step 7

Try to 'get hold of' the day before you start with the children. Good preparation and organization are obviously the key, but 'collecting yourself together' briefly before school starts, looking ahead to likely issues and problems, and doing some simple prediction, may avoid too much crisis management and thinking 'on the run'.

Step 8

Finally, it is useful to cultivate a systematic approach to long-term problem solving and the resolving of difficulties. It is easy to flounder about in a morass of detail, wondering despairingly if there is any answer at all and wasting a great deal of time and energy in the process. Even if you feel, as many experienced teachers do, that they solve problems more by intuition than anything else, there are going to be times when a more organized approach will be much more productive.

Ask yourself:

WHAT is the problem and what specifically are you wanting to achieve in solving it?
WHY do you want to achieve this?
HOW many different ways can you think of which might solve the problem?
DECIDE which of your ways to adopt.
ACT on the decision.

This is perhaps a rather long-winded way of outlining what can become quite a rapid mental process once one gets used to operating it. Writing it down is, however, sometimes more effective than thinking it through.

How to spend time efficiently and productively

I have already indicated that I strongly support a broad definition of achievement, and the four aspects of achievement delineated by the Hargreaves Report (1984) and reaffirmed by the Thomas Report (1985) are a background to what follows.

So, how do we spend time more effectively in the classroom? What are the relative values of class/group/individual teaching? What sort of communication between teacher and child is most effective in terms of learning outcomes? Is it worthwhile to spend a lot of time monitoring and directing children's work? What about time spent keeping records and involving parents? Has the majority of the curriculum 'on offer' got to be 'displayed' at any one time in a primary classroom, or is a more limited focus more effective in terms of children's achievement?

I shall attempt to provide answers to these and other related questions with reference to the important piece of research already mentioned, the ILEA Junior School Project (1986). Its findings are exceptionally important to all primary class teachers although the research was conducted only in junior classes. Some of the findings are obvious, some less so, but they are all backed by convincing evidence.

The study was a longitudinal one and investigated not only cognitive outcomes such as reading and mathematical attainments, but also non-cognitive ones such as behaviour, attitude and motivation, in line with the wider concept of achievement I have already outlined. Careful account was also taken of the different background characteristics of pupils.

What I intend to do in the remainder of this chapter is to discuss those findings involving policy decisions by the classroom teacher which relate favourably to pupil achievement, and which clearly have implications for making the best use of teacher time. These are not to be taken as blueprints for certain success in the classrooms, rather they are signposts which point in the right direction.

The conclusion of the research identifies twelve key factors of effectiveness, of which I have taken eight as having direct implications for how time should be best spent in the classroom. They are not in any particular order of importance and, as will be seen, there are strong interrelationships between most of them. Reference needs to be made to the research findings themselves for the supporting evidence.

Structured sessions

The project findings indicated very clearly that pupils benefited when their school day was structured by the teacher. What does this mean? The structure varied organizationally in different schools, but the factors which led to efficient learning were as follows:

(a) Children's work was generally organized by the teacher.
(b) There was always plenty of work to do.
(c) Pupils were not given extensive responsibility for planning their own work or for choosing work activities.
(d) The structure deliberately allowed the children some choice and freedom.

None of this is perhaps very surprising, and these findings echo those of other researchers who have found that excessive pupil choice is actually disadvantageous to self-esteem as well as to achievement, and that the issue in the classroom is not really one of teacher control versus pupil control, but of teacher control versus lack of control over learning activities. Clearly, time spent structuring the school day is time well spent, but it also seems clear that the class teacher needs deliberately to provide a structure which allows for some pupil choice and control over their work activities. It is obviously important to prepare plenty of work for the children to do, and not to leave this to the developing happenings of the day. Planning also needs to allow for some pupil choice.

Intellectually challenging teaching

This achievement factor is hardly a great surprise. What is specially interesting about the results of the research is that they identify the quality of teacher–child communication as a vital factor in this. We are here at the very core of what a first-class teacher does effectively and spends more time doing than less capable colleagues. Markedly positive effects on pupil achievement occurred when teachers spent a substantial amount of time on 'higher order' questions and statements. What characterizes such questions and statements? To answer this we need to look at some examples.

    (a) 'How do you think the story will end?'
    (b) 'I wonder if there is any other way of weighing those stones?'
    (c) 'Look, those shapes fit together, they tessellate, but these don't seem to'.
    (d) 'Could we find out somewhere what the biggest planet is?'
    (e) 'I don't know how many marbles there are in the tin – you could estimate.'
    (f) 'What do you think we might see at the farm?'

These questions and statements are quite specific, but they also try to involve children more actively in their own learning by inviting different responses and suggesting lines of enquiry. Unfortunately, the teachers observed in the research spent much less time asking questions and making statements of this kind than they did asking 'closed' questions, where a particular response was expected. The report observes that 'over two-thirds of the teachers were observed to make no use of open-ended questions and ... only one per cent of observation time was devoted to questions requiring problem solving'. Similarly, only 1 per cent of observed classroom time was taken up by teachers making 'reasoned or imaginative' statements.

The kind of communication with children that teachers spend much more time on is of the directing and managing kind, telling children what to do and then checking whether they understand what has to be done, rather than discussing or explaining the work itself. This was found to have a negative effect on children's achievement. Rather more surprising is that frequent checking and supervision of the work being done, such as asking pupils how they were getting on, was unproductive in terms of achievement, in contrast to supervision by means of questions and discussions about the work itself. These findings suggest that much of the time teachers spend in communicating with children is simply not productive in terms of achievement. Time is most effectively spent in discussion about the work the children are doing rather than in giving instructions about it. A number of teachers were observed to give few instructions about the work, but the children in their classes knew what they were supposed to be doing and got on with it without constant monitoring. This way of working had positive outcomes in children's achievement.

Work-centred environment

The main characteristic of a work-centred environment appears to be that the teacher and her children spend a substantial amount of time talking about work and actually doing it! As we have already seen, much teacher talk is about management, monitoring and control rather than about the work itself. As one might expect, other characteristics of a work-centred environment are children getting on with their activities, eagerness to start a new task when the previous one is completed, a generally low noise level (but not silence) and movement about the class which generally has to do with the task in hand. Other researchers confirm the crucial importance of communicating with children about their work. Galton *et al.* (1980) say 'all three groups of successful teachers had more task interactions than the typical teacher in the sample', and others have stressed the importance of efficient use of classroom time in this respect.

Limited focus within sessions

The finding that a limited focus within sessions is a key factor in effective learning will probably come as quite a surprise to many teachers. The orthodox view is that a classroom set-up with several different activities in different curriculum areas taking place simultaneously is a sign of skilful and effective teaching. Inexperienced teachers in particular worry very much about this and wonder if they will ever be able to perform this particular juggling act. It also seems that a considerable amount of teacher training is directed towards realizing this ideal. I would suggest that this pattern of work organization is associated in many teachers' minds with the ideal of an effective, practical and workshop-based curriculum. The research findings suggest that more effective learning takes place when teachers devote their attention to one particular curriculum area within a session, or at the most to two. If there are any more than that, pupil progress is measurably hindered. The characteristics of classrooms where work in three or more curriculum areas was going on simultaneously tended, interestingly, to be the opposite ones to those of classrooms which were perceived as very 'work-centred'. That is to say, pupil industry was lower and noise and pupil movement were greater. Communication opportunities between the teacher and the children were reduced and less time was spent in discussing work.

It is also important to point out that the children, even if they were all working in one particular curriculum area, were not doing exactly the same work. Choice of topic and level of difficulty could and did vary within the same curriculum area, which is hardly surprising! The implication of all this for teacher time is that although a multicurriculum area approach within a single session seems to be an efficient use of teacher time, this is apparent rather than real. If teacher time is to be directed towards maximizing achievement, then it is best spent providing appropriate and stimulating work for the children in one or two curriculum areas within a single session.

Maximum communication between teachers and pupils

We have already seen how 'higher order' communication between teacher and child is a crucial factor in achievement. The more the teacher was able to manage matters so that she could increase the number of such communications with her children, the more progress they would make. The project found that most teachers spent the majority of their time with individuals and, on the face of it, this seems the right thing to do. Many of the most powerful images in English primary education (for instance, the classroom as workshop with the master craftsman imparting skills to the apprentice) focus sharply on the individual and imply that the ideal classroom contains individual children who all negotiate their own work programme with their teacher. Some school designs reflected this concept with partitioned work bays and much reduced space for the class as a whole.

Now, clearly, if teachers give most of their attention to talking with individuals, some simple calculations will soon make it clear that in the normal course of events the individual child can expect only a few such contacts during the day. Would it be true to say that 'higher order' communications with children, the ones which lead to increased progress and achievement, can only be effectively made between the teacher and the child in individual conversation? Clearly this is not the case, and the research found that when teachers spoke to the whole class, this made it possible for more higher order communications to be received by all the children. Obvious examples are the reading of a high quality book to the class or a really stimulating and well-organized class lesson. Of course, none of this is to say that individual teacher/child contacts are not important. What the project does confirm is that a balance between class, individual and group contacts between teacher and children was most effective: an important characteristic of successful teaching is accurate judgement in striking that balance, given the particular characteristics and circumstances of the class.

Galton *et al.* (1980) found that the more successful teachers were what they called 'class enquirers', who combined whole-class teaching with individual work. The Thomas Report comments on some highly effective work which was conducted 'by a teacher using exposition and discussion with a group of children or a whole class. Almost always this teaching brought a sense of eagerness and involvement to the work that was less often apparent when children were working on their own'.

The difficulties of managing individual work on a large scale were also noted, with children having to wait their time for individual attention and often having to be directed to 'filler' activities. However, returning to the Junior School Project, it did *not* find that traditional class teaching was the most effective. In fact, the evidence showed that it was not specially beneficial for the children in terms of learning outcomes.

The implications of all this for effective use of teacher time are clear. To spend the great majority of your time in individual contact with the children in your class does not seem to be as effective as a blend of class, group and individual teaching. A serious look at where you strike the balance may well be called for, and you may then feel that you wish to make changes in how you spend your time.

Record keeping

Another finding which has implications for teacher time is the positive effect which results from efficient record keeping. Where teachers kept records which monitored children's work progress and also used their records to inform and develop their teaching, this had, unsurprisingly, a positive effect. Teacher records of children's personal and social development were also found to be beneficial, especially in regard to the wider aspects of achievement already referred to.

Parental involvement

Good teachers have frequently involved parents in their children's education at school and have also tried to encourage parental involvement in their educational progress at home. In a sense, the project, in confirming the value of such efforts, is confirming the obvious, but it is always nice to have research findings corroborate common sense and experience! Activities such as working alongside teachers in class, thus helping to free teacher time for other matters, coming with the class on educational visits and attending parents' meetings to discuss educational progress all have a good effect on children's progress, as does teachers making themselves generally available to parents. It is interesting that parental involvement in the more social or fund raising sense, in a formal PTA, was not found to be a positive factor in effective schooling. I feel very strongly that teacher time spent in involving parents is rarely wasted and will be repaid not only in terms of good relationships but also, if the Junior School Project is right, and it surely is, in terms of effective learning outcomes.

Creating a positive climate

Many factors go towards the creation of a positive climate in a school. Some of these depend on how head and colleagues work together, what they agree on as being important and how they put these agreements into practice. Some, however, are very much the province of the class teacher. It is a great strength of our primary education system that teachers regard relationships with the children in their class as being of central importance to their work, and it is good to have research confirm how important these relationships are in terms of learning outcomes. Encouraging self-control, less punishment and more praise are all positive factors and these do not come as any surprise. What is perhaps less obvious is the important role played by teachers' 'non-school' discussions with children. On the face of it, this seems to contradict another finding, which is the importance of 'higher order' communications with children about their work. The contradiction is more apparent than real. Many such discussions are very high level indeed, and are purposeful educational activities in themselves, in contrast to the routine management and monitoring exchanges between teacher and child which are so wasteful of precious time and so ineffectual in terms of pupil progress and development.

Conclusion

Lack of space prevents me from discussing more. I hope I have used what is available well to fulfil my two original intentions, namely to give some practical hints for class teachers on making more efficient use of their time, and to put forward some research backed findings which seem to indicate a framework within which teachers can spend time more productively with their children.

It is less than half the story to be able to manage your time efficiently. It is more important to spend your time in truly productive ways, ways which promote achievement in the children that you teach. If a class teacher can do both, then her children are very fortunate indeed.

References

Craig I 1987 *Primary School Management in Action*. Longman
Drucker P *The Effective Manager*.
Galton M, Simon B, Croll P 1980 *Inside the Primary Classroom (The Oracle Project)*. Routledge and Kegan Paul
ILEA 1984 *Improving Secondary Schools* (The Hargreaves Report)
ILEA 1985 *Improving Primary Schools* (The Thomas Report)
ILEA 1986 *The Junior School Project*

8 Using other adults in the classroom

Helen Gillespie

In this chapter, I propose to look at the ways in which we, as teachers, can organise the help offered by people such as ancillary staff, students, parents, nursery nurses and other adults, to gain the maximum benefit for the children we teach. It will be necessary to look briefly at some of the advantages to be gained from such help, some of the problems which may be involved and the organisation of such help, which needs to be considered by the class teacher before the collaboration begins.

We must recognise that children who come to us at the beginning of their schooling are an amalgam of all the experience and influences they have met previously. It would be foolish to ignore these factors; it is our task as educators to build upon them and we must welcome any positive help that is offered, channelling it in the right direction to gain the greatest advantage for the children. It may be very testing to have other adults working alongside us in the classroom, but properly organised and with sufficient goodwill on both sides, it can only be a plus factor in the life of the class.

The help offered is sometimes voluntary and at other times professional, but at all times it needs to be structured and has to be viewed within the context of the whole classroom situation. It is our responsibility to liaise efficiently with all the groups who seek to work with us. We must look to the quality of our relationships with them and our direction of them in the carrying out of their 'help'. It is essential to examine the ways in which we can assist in providing them with the necessary skills, techniques and understanding. Time spent in this way with the non-professional helpers will be reflected in the quality of what they subsequently offer to the children. At all times we need to value what they have to give and encourage them to share their enthusiasms and expertise. We have to be sensitive to their needs and to be aware that they may have worries about being involved in what they have traditionally regarded as the class teacher's domain. We must endeavour to make them feel valued for what they can offer.

Obviously, parental involvement is one of the main areas of help available to the school, but many of the stated or underlying principles will apply to everyone who provides assistance in the classroom, professional or non-professional.

Using volunteers in the classroom

The practice of adults other than teachers helping in schools has gradually increased over the years. It appears that in the majority of schools helpers are welcomed for general tasks. Many teachers are glad to accept help in the classroom, and it is this particular help that we will now examine.

Reasons for instigating parental and other volunteer involvement in the classroom

The school's point of view

(a) The volunteer's understanding of the aims and objectives of the school is usually increased considerably by working within the classroom alongside the class teacher.

(b) There is the obvious practical help of 'an extra pair of hands' being available to the teacher.

(c) Added breadth is given to the 'hidden curriculum'.

(d) It becomes possible to provide more individual help for children with special needs.

(e) There is an improvement and extension in the scope of the experiences offered to the children.

(f) Communication and relationships between school and the community are improved.

(g) Children are given the opportunity to see the community and school more closely linked in a positive partnership.

(h) Teachers may gain a better understanding of a particular child and his needs by increasing the communication between themselves and a parent. If the adult involved in helping is not a parent then there are advantages to be gained from an objective 'outsider's' view of the pupil.

The helper's point of view

(a) Increased understanding is gained of the school's aims and objectives, and of its unique problems.

(b) Better understanding of particular children and their needs results.

(c) Extra understanding gained results in more confident handling of their own children.

(d) The experience of working with children within a larger group and a different environment from home is given.

(e) They have the chance to add to their own personal development, e.g. by taking increased responsibility for a particular activity in the classroom or having the opportunity to develop a particular talent or interest.

The importance of training

Problems can arise. Occasionally schools have encountered the situation where volunteer helpers do not have a 'professional' approach to the children and their difficulties. They may, for example, discuss a particular child and his progress or lack of it with others outside the school. In discussing such problems with teachers, they stress the importance of prevention, and the need for helpers to be offered the opportunity to take part in training in the skills and techniques essential if their contribution is to be of value.

It may be helpful at this point to describe a course organised through the auspices of a local teachers' centre in Kent, involving twenty schools in the area and designed to show a group of 'helping' parents and others the philosophy underlying what they were being asked to do in schools. The course was organised by a planning committee comprising several heads, teachers and volunteer helpers, the teachers' centre warden, a teacher from a further education college and a teacher adviser in mathematics.

Six areas of investigation were defined:

1. The value of play
2. Helping with reading
3. The value of mathematical games
4. Cooking activities ⎱ taken together
   Craft activities ⎰
5. School visits
6. Resources.

Important considerations kept in mind by the planning group were:

1. The course was specifically designed for those volunteers already helping in schools, or likely to help in the future.
2. The course components would be aimed at those areas where interested adults were most likely to help.
3. The sessions would suggest rather than instruct.
4. Different venues would make for a cross-fertilisation of ideas.
5. The schools would be divided into geographical groupings so that course members would not have too far to travel.

6. There would be an evaluation and a published paper at the end of the project.

Schools in the project were divided into four groups and a timetable was devised providing six sessions based on the six designated areas of interest and followed by a plenary reporting back session. Each school in the group hosted at least one session. Each session aimed to provide a chance for them to hear some explanation of the educational philosophy underlying the particular area being explored, some time for them to be involved in practical activities and a question and answer time at the end.

The results of a questionnaire which the helpers had filled in after the fifth meeting were analysed and discussed at the plenary session. In general, the members felt that the course had been worthwhile, but obviously there were varying views on the usefulness of different components and suggestions were made as to how improvements could be made in subsequent courses.

There was a general consensus among course members that the obvious next stage was for schools to organise follow-up training activities for their own helpers. The planning committee held several follow-up meetings to prepare a booklet containing:

(a) details of how the course was envisaged;

(b) details of organisation (including timetables, venues, etc.);

(c) a follow-up sheet produced by each tutor under the six headings;

(d) written evaluation of the comments from course members, details of questionnaire sheets and ideas for ways in which follow-up ideas could be implemented.

It was interesting to note that several of the problems which can occur when non-professionals are working alongside teaching staff, e.g. confidentiality and the necessity to treat all the children impartially, arose naturally for discussion and the conclusions were very encouraging. It was hoped that the breadth of information and ideas would offer parents ways of assisting with the development of their own children both at home and at school.

As classroom teachers involved in the education of young children, we have a responsibility to make sure that the experiences we offer to them are of the highest quality. If we are to do our job properly, we have a duty to make use of any area of help or expertise which brings breadth and increased understanding to the curriculum. In the view of many classroom practitioners, this means that we must eagerly and gladly accept the opportunity to involve interested and caring adults in a partnership. As stated in the University of Reading, Centre of Reading document (1983):

On that first morning when a child is led by the hand to school, he carries more than his lunch and PE kit with him. He brings five years of vital experiences, many of which his parents have instigated and shared and it is they who have been the chief influence and educators!

As professionals now involved in the educating of this child, we must be aware of where the child is at and we cannot sever the parental involvement which has been an integral part of his development up to this stage. If the parents are still vitally interested in their child's development, it is only a short step to being involved with the development of other children at school and we need to build on this. We must value them for what they have to offer and seek to give them added understanding of how children develop and how we, as educators, are concerned to make that growth relevant and meaningful.

One parent describes her feelings about her several years of helping in the classroom as follows:

> Having been determined to enjoy my own children's younger years to the full, I have felt extremely fortunate to have had the time to become so involved with primary education in this delightful way. It is hard to judge how much an extra adult may actually contribute in the classroom, as the nature of the role will vary so much from the purely manual help with the time-consuming jobs, to the caring supervision of small groups, to the particular aid of one child with an exceptionally fiddly task. Much time is certainly saved when essential manual tasks are completed by a helper, and certain activities are only feasible with an extra pair of hands, eyes, etc.

At this stage, it may be helpful to mention the children in our schools with very specific 'special needs'. If the help given to these children in any area of the curriculum is to be of value, it must be controlled and monitored by teachers. It is their responsibility to ensure that the experiences offered and the knowledge imparted is relevant to the particular child. This is another very powerful reason for instigating a training programme for voluntary helpers, in order to increase their understanding of the reasons for offering children the experiences that we do and to make their contribution as valuable as possible for the children involved.

Visitors

A very valuable contribution to the stimulation of children's creative energy can be made by a visit from any adult with an interest or talent. An author or an illustrator of children's books will usually evoke great enthusiasm among them. If the children themselves are encouraged to 'publish' their writing, they will very naturally welcome an adult who does the same into the classroom, and gain considerably from the experience.

It is always sensible to prepare the children for such a visit by reading some of the author's works so that the subsequent interaction between class and visitor will be much more relevant. When the author visits there are various ways to organise the event, but, of course, you are restricted by the way in which the visitor prefers to approach it. If they are willing to make their talk to the children just part of the proceedings, then the visit can include a workshop on writing, discussion either in groups or as a class, readings from the author's books which can be dramatised by the children, and even 'publishing' a book at the end of a session under the direction of the author. All of these options and many more which have been suggested will enlarge the class's understanding of how a book is written. When children write, they nearly always see the value of illustrations and a visiting illustrator can stimulate their imaginations whilst giving practical insight into their art.

One class, as part of an 'arts in school' project, had the services of an illustrator who visited once a week. She began by showing the children her pictures in books already published, and then allowed them to watch as she built up a picture for inclusion in a new book. Under her guidance, the children illustrated their own stories which were 'published' for the rest of the class to enjoy. The illustrator initially worked with the whole class and subsequently worked with small groups to facilitate them in working on their own illustrations, suggesting ways of overcoming problems and demonstrating skills and techniques. This was a reversal of the 'write first then illustrate' model; many of these children built up an imaginative picture with many elements and the stories followed quite naturally as a result of explaining them to others.

These examples obviously make use of the help of professionals to stimulate children's interest, but enthusiastic amateurs can also provide invaluable help. We always need to be ready to accept the involvement of any adult who is willing to share their interest. In one school a child's aunt, who created knitted garments from wool 'off the sheep's back' right through to the completed sweater, was willing to demonstrate all the processes involved. She showed the children wool being carded, spun on a spinning wheel, dyed using natural ingredients and, finally, turned into the finished article. This lady not only talked about her work but also made an illustrated book about the stages involved and followed it up by helping a group of children to write and illustrate adventure stories about a picture she had produced on one of her garments. The stories produced were rich in language and content.

At another school, for a day-long seminar on 'other countries' parents of different nationalities were persuaded to run 'workshop' sessions for the pupils on aspects of life in another country. One mother born in Japan demonstrated how to put on a traditional Japanese dress and also showed some traditional Japanese crafts.

Every community is rich in such people, and their help should not be neglected.

Professionals working alongside the teacher

Many teachers now have the benefit of having other professionals working alongside them in the classroom. The special considerations that arise when more than one teacher has full-time collaborative responsibility for a group of children are dealt with elsewhere in this book. Here I will consider help that is offered to teachers who retain the overall professional responsibility for a class.

Ancillary help/welfare assistants

It would appear that in many areas outside the 'special' sector, the incidence of welfare/ancillary help being provided is rapidly decreasing. There seems to be little consensus on how such time can be used most valuably. A study of job descriptions does not help. They vary from those who see the job in terms of physical welfare of children only, e.g. treatment of cut knees, to the other end of the spectrum where 'anything the headteacher may require' seems to be the requirement.

Where people from this group are available to be used within classrooms, many of the ways in which volunteer help has been described will also be applicable to them. In schools where ancillary help is available in the reception class, it should be possible to make use of it for the benefit of any of the new entrants who are finding it difficult to settle down to being part of a large group. It is important for the assistant to build up a good relationship with the classroom teachers and of course to be able to work with them to give maximum help to the children. It appears that ancillary staff are often used to work with less able children under the direction of the teacher. These children will obviously gain in confidence from the one-to-one help received. The ability to work as part of a team is of paramount importance and a good understanding of the educational philosophy of the school is very important indeed if the help given is to be informed and valuable.

Part-time teachers

It would appear that this category of teacher is most often employed to work with children with specific special needs. Increasingly these pupils are being given extra help within their own classroom rather than being withdrawn to another part of the school. It is felt that they will gain most from the extra help if it is offered mainly alongside their peers; 'corridor learning' is not considered to be as helpful. In order for these children to feel that they are functioning as part of a class, it is imperative that they spend most of their time with their classmates. It is obvious that the part-time teacher must have a good working relationship with the class teacher and also with the other children in the class. As there may be a number of part-time teachers visiting any one classroom during the course of a week, there will be a strain on everyone involved unless there is a real desire to make the situation work for the overall benefit of the children. Many part-time teachers have stressed that they see 'home visiting' as an integral part of their responsibilities. The increased knowledge and understanding of the children's backgrounds, needs and problems must be shared with the class teacher and hopefully the quality of experiences subsequently offered to the children in school will be made increasingly relevant.

The organisation of the visiting teacher's time is, of course, a decision for individual schools but some principles must surely apply to every situation:

1. The class teacher and the part-time teacher must discuss the needs of the pupil(s) involved and decide strategies together for ensuring that there is progress.
2. There needs to be constant evaluation of what is offered, including planned procedures for review and assessment, to make sure that it is relevant. This requires the collaboration of both teachers.
3. There must be tolerance and understanding on both sides of the difficulties encountered in working in the same room with, at times, different priorities.
4. Pupils must be made aware that the teacher has a real understanding of the fact that their cultural backgrounds and values are an important part of what they bring to school.

One teacher working with ESL children has described how she organises the help she offers. She has been asked to work with a small group of children in six classes spread throughout the primary school. This means that she is involved with each group for two sessions per week (a session lasts approximately an hour and a half) and she also spends one session each week 'home visiting' the parents of her pupils. She sees her relationships with the class teachers as of paramount importance and has worked very hard at building a solid foundation of mutual trust and appreciation. This has involved meeting for informal and formal meetings within school, social meetings outside school hours' and attending in-service courses with the school staff. She has involved an ancillary helper in speaking and writing Bengali to benefit some of her pupils and also to communicate with their parents. During her classroom sessions, she naturally prefers to use her own interests and expertise in science, environmental studies, and art and craft, but always sees these in the context of what the class as a whole is studying. Her group may, perhaps, make a large book based on 'pets'. Each child will make a contribution, e.g. a picture, some writing, an audio tape about the subject, a model or collage. The individual items will be labelled in English and in the child's first language. Often, a photograph of the child is put into the book. She considers one of the most important stages to be the sharing of this book, and the experiences of making it, with the rest of the class. This gives the ESL pupil a chance to feel that their contribution is valued, and the subsequent boost to self-confidence is often immediately visible.

With the encouragement of the class teacher, she has created a small environment within the classrooms in which she strives to share her work, and that of the pupils she helps. It can be seen that this particular teacher views herself very much as part of a team and the work she does with her group as an integral part of the learning of the class as a whole. Hopefully, the classroom teachers she works alongside see her contribution as valuable and appreciate the fact that she is complementing everything they offer to their class and making it relevant to the children.

Sharing work that has been done under the direction of the 'special needs' teacher is a very positive influence for good and will help these children to be viewed by the rest of the class as important. One school reported that a 'special needs' group together devised a short play and cast it using all the members of their class, directed it themselves and shared it with parents. It was a great success and the less able children were given great credibility in the eyes of their peers.

Students

It is obvious that the value of help offered by students will depend on their stage of training, individual expertise and special interests. When working in the classroom alongside the class teacher, they need to be carefully directed but it is also necessary for the teacher to be sensitive to the students' desire to experiment and find their own way of approaching teaching. Students must be given help to make sure that this development of their individual 'style' is not in any way going to cause problems for the pupils they are working with. They need to be shown good classroom practice and encouraged to aim for excellence themselves. This is probably best done by a gradual increase in involvement with the teaching of the children, beginning with observation, followed by individual involvement with a particular child or small group of children and culminating with the student taking the entire class for a specified time on a particular topic. If their professional development is to be considered, there must be assessment and evaluation at all stages. This can take the form of informal 'chats' at playtimes, during the midday breaks and after school as to how a particular involvement with the children succeeded or failed and why. It is also necessary to arrange formal, regular times for the teacher and student to discuss progress.

As with all other adults helping children in the classroom, students must first develop the ability to relate well to the class teacher and other members of staff, both professional and non-professional, and most important of all, to the children in the class in which they are working.

Nursery nurses

When entering a nursery class, it is often impossible to identify which is the teacher and which the nursery nurse. This is just how it should be; there really should be no demarcation lines in the involvement with the children. However, the difference will be that the teacher will take ultimate responsibility for planning the organisation, curriculum and day-to-day running of the nursery class. It would be a foolish teacher, however, who did this in isolation and failed to involve the nursery nurse at every stage in the proceedings. Her training, expertise and skills are such that she has a very valuable contribution to make to the education of nursery children. She will have a good understanding of the stages of development through which the 3–5-year-old should pass and the sensitive nursery teacher will make sure that this is fully used for the benefit of the children.

On a day-to-day basis, the nursery nurse will be involved in making preparations for the day ahead, setting out activities, preparing materials, etc., and facilitating children in all their work. She will be fully involved in encouraging the language development of these young children by her informed intervention in the play. She will take full part in all the activities which happen through the day in a nursery class under the sensitive direction of the nursery teacher. Like all other adults helping in the classroom, she must be encouraged to offer of her expertise and made to feel that her very real contribution is valued by the 'other staff'. In some nursery classes, the nursery nurse is only involved with the physical well-being of the children, but this would seem to be a very short-sighted approach. Most nursery teachers are well aware of the degree of understanding that a well-trained nursery nurse will have, and of the invaluable help they have to offer to young children. Their training will make them valuable members of the nursery team, well able to offer children all the experiences which are important at different stages in their development.

Conclusion

There can be no doubt that informed help in the classroom, either professional or non-professional, monitored carefully by the class teacher, can positively contribute to the quality of what is offered to pupils. If this help is to be as valuable as possible, schools need to look into the possibility of organising 'in-school' training in the necessary skills and techniques. There may also be advantages to be gained in teaching staff working together to draw up a list of ways in which classroom help can be utilised most successfully.

References

University of Reading School of Education 1983 *Parents in Partnership*

9 Developing real-life learning

John Bird

'My hope is that through the gradual weakening of the constraints of schooling, we will so loosen its fabric and so strengthen the opportunities to learn from other sources, that it will become impossible to separate learning from life and student and teacher from friends learning together. For this we need a real flowering of other options'

Ronald Gross (1980)

It is very difficult indeed to avoid learning. For all people, whatever their age, it takes place almost all of the time wherever the individual is and whatever the individual is doing. We know from our own experience that it takes place most effectively when the learning is both active and relevant to the learner.

The purpose of school learning in this lifelong learning process must therefore be to provide motivation, support and direction to the learner; to help with the acquisition of necessary skills and to provide a model for learning. Most important of all, schools must, in order to be able to fulfil this function, be 'of the real world' and therefore break down what Ferguson (1980) calls 'the windowless walls that have closed off school from community, from the milieu of real life'. Real-life schools are dynamic, organic groups of people who consiantly seek to provide learners with relevant learning opportunities. Although we generally refer to children as the learners in the primary school, it is important to remember that the learner is in fact anyone, teacher, child or any other person involved in the school.

In order to attain this real-life state, schools must in their organisation and curriculum constantly take account of changes occurring in the real world and the ways in which these changes affect the learning needs of children.

Look at the list below. How do you think these recent changes have changed the learning needs of children?

Figure 9.1

Changes in society	Changed learning need
Increased family mobility and consequent change in the frequency and variety of social contacts	
Accessibility of the media	
Changing patterns of employment	
Changing patterns of work and increased leisure time	
Improved system of communication	
The knowledge explosion	
Increasing materialism	
The changing roles of men and women	
The developing use of computers and robotics	
The exhaustion of traditional sources of energy	
World pollution	
Rapid development of technology – moving the power base to the young?	
The development of a multicultural society	
Problems of drugs, Aids, etc.	
Increasing centralisation of power in government, business and service industries	

Further to these more specific changes in our society and their consequent effect upon children's learning needs, children need to learn how to cope with the fact that the rate of change in their world is accelerating – constant, rapid change is here to stay! In order to cope, children need to acquire new, relevant skills. As Toffler (1971) suggests, 'people who must live in super industrial societies will need new skills in three crucial areas: learning, relating and choosing'.

The average amount of time which a child spends in school varies between 13 per cent and 17 per cent of the year. Since learning is a lifelong process it follows that a great deal more learning occurs outside school than inside it. This simple fact and its consequences needs to be more willingly recognised by teachers and parents in the ways in which they both provide learning opportunities for children.

If education is to recognise that the changing needs of children must be reflected in changing views of educational provision, in order to develop real-life learning, there seem to be three major requirements. First, in the organisation of the school account needs to be taken of children's changed learning needs and the school's role needs to be adapted accordingly. Second, schools need to develop a real-life approach to the curriculum which better reflects the changing needs of children. Third, the responsibility for learning must be shared between teacher, parent and child.

Let us now examine the practical implications of these three consequences for the teacher.

The real-life school

The traditional view of the school is of an establishment which children attend in order to do their learning. The expectation seems to be that children will acquire skills, knowledge and attitudes and that the responsibility for the acquisition of these lies with the teacher. This view of schooling is contrary to the needs of children. Parents, teachers and children need to view the school very differently if it is to function effectively as a contributory part of lifelong learning.

1. *School as a learning base*

School is not a complete, closed learning environment. It should be a catalyst which provides starting points for learning and the motivation to learn. The directions and the necessary enquiry can then be followed both inside and outside the school in time and place. The school can provide the resources, expertise and encouragement to support the learning and act as a constant reference point during the learning.

2. School as a learning model

We have seen that children need to learn how to learn. Part of the school's role is to help children acquire the necessary skills, concepts and attitudes which form the learner's tools for learning. For example, the child needs to acquire the skills shown in Figure 9.2, amongst others, in order to learn effectively.

Figure 9.2

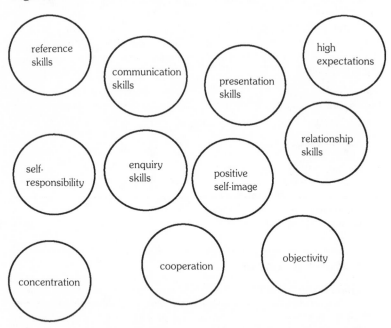

The school's curriculum, organisation and methods should be planned to develop those skills and thereby provide children with a model for learning which they can apply to their learning wherever and whenever it occurs.

3. School as a caring community

School should exemplify what it seeks to promote in learners. Sharing and caring should be the 'norm'. Within the school community, the quality of interpersonal relationships should have highest priority. Empathy and understanding should be qualities demonstrated by all people involved and the highest possible standards of behaviour and achievement from learning should be expected by everyone.

4. *School as a learning centre for all*

All people are learners, whatever their age. The primary school with its unique closeness to its community can facilitate learning and personal growth in all people. Resources, facilities and expertise abound both within the primary school and its community. The school's function should extend beyond the child of statutory school age to all people. Indeed by so doing, the learning opportunities available to those of statutory school age are greatly enriched and broadened.

At this point it may be interesting to examine the implications of these four characteristics of the real-life school for the teacher and the organisation of classroom learning. How would you complete the following table?

Figure 9.3

	Myself	My classroom
School as a learning base		
School as a learning model		
School as a caring community		
School as a learning centre for all		

The real-life curriculum

The curriculum which we offer to our learners has hardly changed for a century or more. It is still largely based on the notion that there exists a body of knowledge which must be transmitted and that this body of knowledge occurs in neat compartments called subjects.

The origins of this lie in a society which was characterised by stability, rigidity, routine and order. Our present society is characterised by none of these things. The curriculum which we offer to our children is, to a large extent, divorced from their experience of life, not relevant to them and in no way designed to equip them for either their present or future needs. Too often the curriculum which we offer is boring, repetitive, passive and, worst of all, irrelevant to the child. It is, as Mark Hewlett (1987) wrote, 'poorly organised to promote either enjoyment of learning or academic exploration'.

It is increasingly urgent that we view both learning and the learner in holistic terms and stop separating subject from subject, feelings from facts, the learner from the learning. Our curriculum needs to relate learning more closely to the children's experience of life both in its content, its skills and its processes. It should offer opportunities for learners to become involved in real life and thereby develop as people who are able to function in and contribute to society.

Here are three areas in which the teacher can develop a relevant real-life curriculum.

1. *The learning environment*

The traditional learning environment is, for the learner, generally passive, directed and conditioning. For many it results in the development of learned helplessness. Today's learner needs to develop confidence, autonomy and the ability to relate to others. The learning environment needs to:

- Be learner-centred. Shift the emphasis from teaching to learning in order to provide the child with opportunities to take on responsibility for learning.
- Encourage experimenting and risk-taking. Provide opportunities and support for children to try things out, take risks and learn from doing so.
- Not avoid mistake-making. We too often emphasise ticks rather than crosses. Children are afraid to make mistakes. In real life we constantly learn from our mistakes. Remove this fear in children and ensure that mistake-making is seen as a learning experience.
- Offer opportunities to make choices. All areas of life have value implications. It is increasingly important that children are helped to develop the ability to make value choices. This ability needs to be nurtured from very simple beginnings at a very early age.
- Promote high expectations and high standards. The self-fulfilling prophecy really does work. Low expectations will produce low achievements. High expectations can produce incredible things! This is true of both the self and the teacher. Be positive and optimistic with children. Encourage them to expect to do well and to succeed and help them to cope with the very occasional failure too!
- Offer opportunities to learn with others. Learning in a group helps to develop skills of interaction, communication, cooperation and

conflict-resolution. Make group-focused learning a regular part of your teaching strategy. It will be referred to later.
- Offer opportunities to learn through experience. Learning is most meaningful when it is active. Make your curriculum a practical, investigative, living programme.
- Be everywhere, not confined to the school. School-based learning should support the view that learning is a lifelong, universal process.

All of the characteristics of the learning environment listed above are very positive, supportive and necessary parts of a real-life curriculum and vital to the kind of learning which follows.

2. Action and involvement

All of the child's learning should begin in his experience of life. In this sense the child is the curriculum. It is vital that learning springs from a growing awareness of self and the immediate world but also that learning adds to and continues to develop these things. Therefore learning must relate to these things or it is pointless and irrelevant.

Here are four points worthy of consideration in attempting to relate the curriculum to the child's needs.

(a) *Always attempt to relate any school learning to real life* The Cockroft Report states that:

All children need experience of practical work which is directly related to activities of everyday life . . . . Children cannot be expected to be able to make use of their mathematics in everyday situations unless they have the opportunity to experience these situations for themselves.

How often in classrooms can children be observed repeatedly rehearsing skills in total isolation from their application in real life? A great deal of time is still spent, as Barker-Lunn (1984) reminds us, operating in this way, mainly practising mathematical computation and comprehension skills. It seems true also of painting, writing and many other learning activities. How often are children engaged upon observational drawing or writing with a real purpose? Teachers who facilitate real-life learning know that the most effective learning is exciting and relevant to the child. They ensure that it is so and the results are apparent in the children's absorption and in the excellence of their efforts.

(b) *Plan class projects designed to help learners develop knowledge and understanding of their immediate and world community* Project work is, of course, an excellent vehicle for holistic education, for relevant learning and for active learning.

This is the first of two levels of project work which involve the

children in out-of-school learning. It is a popular and well used form of
learning and requires the children to examine such topics as:

> people who help us, myself, the post office, shops and shopping, homes,
> the street, the church, traffic, houses, litter, farming, the school, habitats,
> the weather.

Such projects involve the planned acquisition of skills, concepts and
attitudes across the curriculum and are designed to help children
develop knowledge of the local and extended communities. Many
models exist for the preparation of such projects. I like the simple but
effective model produced by the Development Education Centre
(1985):

What is
the content?

What methods   What do I hope
and resources   the children
shall I use?   will gain?

These kinds of projects are valid and important in the child's
learning since they provide a sound, relevant base of understanding
and a high level of real-life involvement too.

(c) *Involve the children in practical, investigative projects about
real-life issues which result in action concerning the issue*   At this
second level the children's learning becomes action-centred. It
involves them in:

- investigating real issues which are of concern to people;
- taking part in action on behalf of the issue;
- taking increasing responsibility for the direction of the learning;
- developing a sense of community, a 'feel' for people and a sense of
  shared responsibility for the environment;
- becoming increasingly self-empowered, realising through action that
  they are powerful both individually and collectively and can affect the
  quality of life.

The nature of the projects is somewhat different from those at the
first level, the emphasis being upon issues, involvement and action.
For example, one school staff 'brainstormed' ideas for community-
based projects and came up with these:

noise	employment	disability
amenities	interdependence	ageing
lifestyles	comparing communities	loneliness
friendship	designing communities	empty space
energy	pollution	conserving

Each of these offers opportunities for in-depth investigation and for some kind of resultant action which raises the individual and collective awareness and may affect, for some, the quality of life.

The project idea on disability produced the following outline plan.

What do I hope the children will gain?

- an understanding of disability and how it affects people;
- self-awareness and relationship skills through a range of cross-curricular activities in context;
- integration with disabled people and a commitment to achieving equal opportunities for them.

What is the content?

- disability awareness exercises leading to an exploration of feelings;
- an investigation of local access for disabled people;
- an investigation of amenities for disabled people;
- an investigation of the national and international situations;
- spend time learning with local groups who can help raise awareness, e.g. studio theatre;
- form link with local school for the disabled, spend time together, produce joint concert;
- investigate historical treatment of the disabled;
- design aids for the disabled;
- take action as a local pressure group for change with regard to disabled people.

What methods and resources shall I use?

- high proportion of time to be given to group-focused learning;
- considerable amount of role play and 'feelings' work;
- identification of local disabled people;
- school therapists;
- optician;
- visits to other schools, studio theatre;
- video camera.

There are several important points to make about these kinds of projects.

It is vital that the children's involvement in real-life learning should be placed in a global context. Community-based learning must relate to the world. For example, a study of local employment should always be placed in the international context so that comparisons can be made with, for example, third-world countries and conclusions drawn.

Furthermore, there will always be a multitude of world problems worthy of study. For example:

The decay of Venice (I involved a class in a project on this thirteen years ago!)

The Bhopal disaster
The Chernobyl disaster
Acid rain

It is important to the children's needs that projects involve an element of future studies. Part of our purpose in education is to help children plan their own futures and cope with what happens to them. We should help them to see the problems of today and ensure through awareness and action that those problems are solved. Prediction and planned action is vital learning which we should build into learning opportunities.

Two techniques are worthy of special mention as means of facilitating action projects.

First, photography is increasingly used as a method of helping children choose, order and discuss their community. Many schools now have darkrooms and equipment which enable them to become more involved. Photography can provide excellent starting points in investigative projects. Easily operated cameras are necessary and with them children can photograph likes, dislikes and activities. Their results can then form excellent starting points for investigation and action. Second, the Education for Neighbourhood Change Unit at Nottingham University produces excellent packs for use by schools and communities. The packs, based around such themes as living space, planning for real and building design, enable children to organise their investigations, build three-dimensional models of communities and become involved in planning and decision making.

Finally, an increasing number of good curriculum project ideas and materials are being produced from a wide range of sources. Some are listed at the end of this chapter.

(d) *Develop a partnership between school and community* It is important to remember that the community is not some kind of learning zoo into which children venture to walk and gawk. To the children it is often their entire world. Real-life schools and real-life teachers are aware that the relationship between themselves and the community should be empathetic, close and dynamic. School and community are one.

3. *Personal growth*

For many years we have spoken and written very comfortably about the 'hidden curriculum', that area of learning concerned with personal development. We have hoped that children would acquire the skills and attitudes contained within it and have generally not set objectives or planned activities for their acquisition as we do for mathematics or language or geography. Yet is is precisely this area of the curriculum, concerned with personal growth, which is of vital importance to the child of today or tomorrow. Those learners who can be helped to acquire skills in interpersonal relationships and the self-awareness to take greater control of their lives are the ones who will cope most effectively with the world. Instead of leaving personal development to chance, schools should organise the curriculum, the timetable and the facilities in such a way that personal development is a planned and progressive part of the school's purpose.

Here are three areas in which the teacher can develop learning activities in human relations.

(a) *Some on-going activities*   The development of a positive self-image is extremely important and there are a large number of strategies which help develop it. For example:

- Super-person badges. The child is awarded a 'Super-person' badge for success in the area of relationships, not for academic success. The objective is for others to ask why the badge is being worn. The child then feels good when explaining the reason.
- A classroom 'success book' offers children the opportunity to write about and put into a large display folder any item of personal success. The book is frequently referred to and good feelings ensue.
- Display picture-frames can be mounted in busy places to display examples of children's learning in art, writing, etc. The regular changing of the items displayed can form part of 'show and tell' assemblies where children show and explain their efforts to peers, parents and others. The emphasis is upon high individual standards.

Children need to be given regular and frequent opportunities to acquire human relations skills by practising them and therefore the teacher should create opportunities within learning situations for practice to occur. For example:

- Give the children responsibility over a wide range of activities which involve relationships, taking messages, delivering the class register, asking questions, learning with a wide range of people of all ages.
- Perhaps most important of all, the organisation for learning within the classroom should regularly involve group-focused learning. This technique helps develop group skills in interaction, communication, cooperation and conflict resolution. It shifts the emphasis from teaching to learning. It is characterised by:
  - i a group task/objective which presents a group challenge
  - ii children working together to achieve the objective.

The teacher should:
  - i give clear, precise instructions to the group
  - ii resist telling the group how to tackle the task but explain exactly what the task is
  - iii debrief the group at the end of the activity – feedback is very important to the process
  - iv match the challenge to the stage of development of the group.

(b) *Human relations on the timetable*   A growing number of schools have now established for themselves a creative arts room where there is very little furniture, where there are facilities for lighting changes and blackout and where the floor is carpeted. Such a room offers excellent opportunities for children to regularly experience role play, fantasy and a wide range of other human relations activities. The number of books available giving very practical ideas to teachers for human relations activities with primary school children is rapidly growing. A list is included at the end of this chapter.

(c) *Human relations projects*   We saw earlier that project work which involves the children in action is very important to the real-life curriculum. Class projects can also be specifically designed to develop human relations skills. It may be useful to consider these and add to the list:

change, celebrating, treasures/possessions, communicating, families, neighbours, me.

A rapidly growing number of teachers and schools are becoming involved in the area of human relations since it is becoming increasingly obvious that in order to provide for children's educational needs skills in this area are vitally important.

Educational partnership

The third consequence of a commitment to real-life education is that of educational partnership. This is an immense area for discussion and activity but it is important to make some points here for the consideration of the teacher.

A commitment to lifelong learning, with all that it implies, is inevitably a commitment to a view of education as an activity for which the responsibility is shared between parent, teacher and child.

Figure 9.4

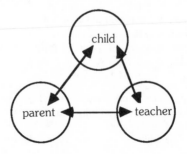

Sharing presents opportunities for all three of the partners to broaden their traditional role in order to relate learning to life. Let us briefly examine these opportunities.

1. *The teacher*

We have seen that teachers increasingly need to shift the emphasis away from themselves towards the learner and take on the role of facilitator. Carl Rogers (1982) has written that if he were to select or train teachers who would be most effective in facilitating learning and personal growth, his criteria would be:

- those who had the ability to be good listeners, who could most readily understand the world as perceived by the student.
- those who tended to feel a warm caring and respect for each student as a unique person.
- those who were secure enough to be themselves with the students; who were not role players but real persons.
- those who tended to believe that persons are, at the core, constructive, not evil.

Teachers who display these personal and attitudinal qualities are those who would be able to share the responsibility for learning with children and parents and who would be able to act as facilitators of learning rather than as didactic teachers. Such teachers believe that initiative is more important than knowledge, and responsibility more important than duty. Their teaching methods and qualities will include:

- a variety of approaches including a commitment to group-focused learning;
- offering a variety of choices to the child;
- good match of activities to developmental stage of the individual;
- learning alongside the children, operating from amongst them;
- an active classroom where children move freely around;
- emphasis on encouragement, praise and co-operation;
- few behavioural problems, children absorbed in activities;
- negotiating learning activities, times and programmes with the child.

Such teachers know that they are not autonomous and that they function most effectively as part of a school team. They recognise that an increasingly important part of their professional role is forming close relationships with parents through:

- home visiting
- regular meetings for shared discussion and goal-setting
- workshops to explain the school's approach and reach shared decisions
- listening very carefully.

Such teachers also know that a commitment to these things changes but in no way diminishes their professionalism.

2. *The parent*

We are all aware of the traditionally minimal role which parents have played in the education of their children. A commitment to real-life learning changes this role and determines that the parent becomes an educator. This implies a commitment to:

- spending time at school
- sharing in the decision-making
- accepting the out-of-school educational role
- listening very carefully
- acquiring some techniques
- developing awareness and understanding of school learning.

3. *The child*

Hopefully, the major implication for the child is that home and school will be very close together in aims and understanding and that therefore the child can enjoy less conflict, greater security and support. It must also offer the child the opportunity to negotiate learning patterns and take on greater self-responsibility.

Educational partnership is an emerging area of study and activity in education. A great deal more could be discussed but space does not permit.

Conclusion

Relating what happens in the classroom to the real lives of children and having the vision to be constantly aware of children's changing needs is extremely difficult to maintain, given the demands of the job. In order to provide the kind of education which is fitted to the needs of children we must make it relevant to their experience of the real world in which they and the school exist.

References

Ronald Gross 1980 in Ferguson M *The Aquarian Conspiracy*. Paladin
Ferguson M 1980 *The Aquarian Conspiracy*. Paladin
Toffler A 1971 *Future Shock*. Pan
Hewlett M 1987 The explicit curriculum *Times Educational Supplement* 2 January 1987

DES 1982 *Mathematics Counts: Reports of the Committee of Inquiry into the Teaching of Mathematics under the Chairmanship of Dr W H Cockcroft.* HMSO

Barker Lunn J 1984 Junior school teachers: their methods and practices *Educational Research*, vol 26 no 3

Development Education Centre 1985 *Theme Work*

Rogers C 1982 *The Effective Teacher, a Person-Centred Guide.* PAVIC publications

Further reading

These books and sources may be useful in considering the real-life curriculum.

Fisher, Hicks 1985 *World Studies 8–13 Handbook.* Oliver and Boyd

Education for Neighbourhood Change Unit, School of Education, University of Nottingham, Nottingham NG7 2RD

Development Education Centre, Selly Oak Colleges, Bristol Road, Birmingham B29 6CE

Community Service Volunteers (Publications Dept), 237 Pentonville Road, London N1 9NJ

Help the Aged Education Dept, 218 Upper Street, London N1

Community Education Development Centre, Briton Road, Coventry CV2 4LF

World Studies Centre, York University, York YO1 5DD

Green Teacher, Llys Awel, 22 Hesl Pentrerheydn, Machynlleth, Powys, Wales SY20 8DN

These books are concerned with human relations. Many are American but they are available from most bookshops.

Ballard J 1982 *Circlebook.* Irvington Publishers, New York

Avery 1978 *Friendly Classroom for a Small Planet.* Avery Publishing Group, New Jersey

Harmin M 1976 *Got to be me.* Argus Communications

Fox C Lynn 1980 *Communicating to Make Friends.* B L Winch Associates

Canfield, Wells 1976 *100 Ways to Enhance Self-Concept in the Classroom.* Prentice-Hall Inc

Masheder M 1986 *Let's Co-operate.* Peace Education Project

Hendricks, Wills 1975 *The Centering Book.* Prentice-Hall Inc

Leech N, Wooster A 1986 *Personal and Social Skills, a Practical Approach for the Classroom.* Religious and Moral Education Press

10 Classroom planning

Ian Craig

The teaching profession is constantly being bombarded with directives and recommendations to manage its affairs more efficiently. It is not uncommon to hear criticisms of the education service in general, and of particular schools, for not knowing the direction in which they are going. Education makes headline news, and parents are becoming more knowledgeable and articulate about it.

Some teachers, many with laudable ideals, have been the profession's worst enemy in the new atmosphere of educational debate, either being unable to justify the directions in which they are going, or making comments such as 'the last thing we want to be is efficient' (Haigh, 1987).

The government has reacted to this 'high profile' by publicizing a wide range of proposals for the reform of the service. I have heard one eminent educationist recently state that we should welcome this government 'interference' and public debate, and turn it to our own advantage. It is a tribute to teachers that the general public now realizes that education is so important. The atmosphere is now right for an unprecedented move forward in the education service.

Many teachers are unhappy about some of the proposals now being publicly discussed, but most would agree that there is a need for structured direction to their work.

At this time of thought about direction, when the whole of the education service is looking towards its aims, and more and more schools are moving towards structured plans for development (ILEA, 1985; House of Commons, 1986), it is perhaps timely to discuss what has generally been an undervalued and neglected aspect of teachers' work – an aspect on which there has been very little published material.

This chapter will attempt to justify why it is necessary for a teacher *formally* to plan her work, what sort of plans are of most value, and finally, to suggest a model of planning for teachers to examine and possibly adapt for their own use.

Why plan?

All teachers plan their work, but this planning is seldom clearly structured once the teacher completes her initial training. Where formal planning does take place, it is often not developed beyond the requirements of the initial training establishment.

Several investigations in the US (reported by Calderhead, 1984), 'have suggested that most of the planning in which teachers engage is fairly informal – *mental planning*' and that

> most of teachers' planning has been found to focus on the preparation of particular lessons. For these, teachers rarely produce sophisticated written plans, though McCutcheon (1980) found that brief notes and 'memory joggers' were common, and would generally involve a listing of topics to be covered, or the books to be used and exercises to be done.

There is good reason to believe that similar conclusions would be drawn from similar surveys in the UK.

Where planning does take place it tends to be incremental rather than rational. It is not uncommon for teachers to consider an overall framework for their work at the beginning of each year, or even at the beginning of each term. These plans are seldom more than very broad frameworks, and provide little structure for the work. They tend to be interpreted in an intuitive rather than a systematic way, and in terms of activities that are to take place rather than of the outcomes that the teacher expects.

Planning therefore tends to be imprecise. The ILEA Junior School Project (1986) found that in the most successful schools, 'the provision of an adequate structure to the school day and ensuring a sufficient degree of teacher direction of work activities, is beneficial for promoting progress and development'. Structure needs to be planned – it does not just happen.

Adequate structure means good management of the child's and the teacher's time. Richardson (1984) states that 'teachers tend to be less 'system-conscious' than those in many other professions'. Some teachers even seem to be proud of this. If teachers are to be respected for their professionalism then they must begin to show that they are able to offer a unique set of skills to the children under their control.

Systematic planning by the teacher does seem to be equated with positive learning outcomes. For materials to be collected together, visits to be organised, and a general balance of activities to be experienced by the children, it is essential that the programme of work is organized in advance.

If continuity of learning is to take place, a systematic plan must also be available for use by 'relief' teachers whenever they are employed, or vital days can be lost to the child's education when such teachers just 'fill in'. Detailed plans also serve as a record for subsequent teachers, who are easily able to establish what aspects of particular subjects have been previously covered.

In DES (1987) it is stated that:

> In all examples of good practice the educational objectives were firmly established ... This clear view of objectives had not in any way reduced the flexibility of the teaching arrangements. On the contrary it had provided a sure base from which the educational opportunities arising as the work progressed were taken up and used to advantage while the pace and thrust of the work were maintained ... the overriding characteristic is that of clear aims and purposeful teaching.

It is my belief that teachers need clearly thought-out aims for *all* that they do within the classroom, and that the resulting teaching should be purposefully planned.

Isn't it a lot of work?

I don't think so, and my belief is borne out by teachers who have tried systematic planning, who find that once they have got into such a planning pattern it takes a lot less time than they had anticipated. They also find that well thought-out planning gives them greater confidence in the classroom as they feel more in control of what is going on, and this in turn leads to them being more relaxed. This has positive effects on the children, and on the quality of the work that takes place. Teachers then begin to report a greater job satisfaction.

What sort of plans?

If planning is going to serve the functions outlined above, what sort of plans should they be?

Again, in DES (1987) HMI advise us that:

> Knowledge, skills, concepts and attitudes are seen as four key elements of learning to be acquired. The curriculum in English primary schools has frequently been discussed in terms of activity and experience, yet the good practice observed suggests that these terms are too limiting and express only a partial view.

Planning should always start from the point of identifying what knowledge, skills, concepts and attitudes we want the child to achieve and understand. We then need to determine how far he is already along the road to this achievement and understanding. Good planning is always a sensible mixture of identifying where the child is and where the teacher wants to take him to.

It has been consistently stressed that where good practice is observed there is a clear continuity in approach and planning throughout the school (ILEA, 1985; House of Commons, 1986; ILEA, 1986; DES, 1987). Systematic planning should therefore, if possible, be a school-wide activity, and should be collaborative and cooperative. However, if only one teacher in a school sees the value of a detailed approach to planning, it is better for her systematically to plan alone, than not at all.

Teachers should, if possible, discuss their ideas both formally and informally with colleagues, and have the facilities to plan specific activities together. When deciding upon aims and objectives it is often valuable to discuss them with colleagues to ascertain whether your views are consistently held by others. Both the plans themselves and the planning process can valuable be shared.

Shared planning allows others on the staff, some specialists in particular curricular areas, others with particular interests and expertise, to contribute ideas and also to see what is being planned. It may be that colleagues have particular resources that they can share, and it is much better to plan their use into the work than to discover their availability during the course of the activity. Collaborative planning allows full use to be made of available resources.

Have you ever discussed a classroom activity that has already taken place with a colleague, only to be told by her that a relevant piece of equipment that you did not know to be in the school was in her room? Have you ever gone to the school's resources room to collect a piece of equipment or a book that you knew was there, and been unable to find it because it was already being used, you and a colleague having planned its use on the same day? Collaborative planning can avoid these pitfalls.

Collaboration and cooperation are also valuable at the review stage, when the planned work has taken place. A sharing of problems and successes will help you and your colleagues to benefit from the experiences.

Some teachers may also wish to share the work itself, planning a theme cooperatively, teaching it together, and even watching and later commenting on each other's work.

Learning should not be left to chance. Before planning an activity for children, the teacher should ask herself the following questions:

What learning is to take place?

    i Why?
    ii What will the children know or be able to do as a result?
    iii How will I know that learning has taken place?
  Which children are to take part?
  Over what period of time?

It is *not* possible to plan work *in detail* for every child in the class, and to supervise and measure *all* the outcomes. It is, however, possible to work on particular planned activities with specific groups of children, when planning *can* be detailed and outcomes can be identified.

Teachers cannot hope to supervise closely every activity that takes place in a modern primary classroom. Where they try to do this the result is what Calderhead (1984) calls 'busyness'. Because of the teacher's preoccupation with ensuring that every child is 'busy' or occupied, no time is left for 'teaching'; she is constantly moving from one child to another, dealing with problems but never 'focusing' her attention on any one child for more than a few seconds at a time.

The secret of good classroom planning is to make sure that whenever an activity is taking place with one group of children that is 'costly' of teacher time, the majority of the other children are engaged in tasks that they can do with little attention. It is for the teacher, when planning her work, to bear 'balance' in mind. In every area of the curriculum, there are new activities that need to be introduced by the teacher, and consolidation and practice activities can be planned for the child needing little teacher help.

In my judgement, a well-planned classroom would generally have a number of activities taking place at the same time, all of them planned for, possibly on different areas of the curriculum, but not necessarily so. At least one group of children may be receiving 'focused' teaching from the teacher, possibly on the introduction of a new skill. Other children in the class would be undertaking activities that need little teacher involvement, possibly practising skills that had been taught to them in previous focused sessions. All the children not in the 'focused' group would know that they should not disturb the teacher unless really necessary. The planning that the teacher had undertaken for the focused teaching is much more detailed than for the other activities.

In this way, as the week progresses, *every* child receives either individual or small group *teaching* on a number of occasions. Because of the small group relationship, the teacher is easily able to assess progress.

These focused sessions do not preclude the teacher from using whole-class techniques where she thinks that they are appropriate, nor does it place excessive demands on her planning. It will often be the case that she will decide that a whole day (or more) may be required to teach a particular new skill to the whole class in focused-group sessions. Only one plan will be needed for this activity although it will be varied from group to group depending on their needs.

This kind of classroom organization and planning enables the teacher to spend planned periods of time with each child at regular intervals. In a modern, busy primary classroom, it is often the case that *no* time is spent teaching the individual. When much of the planning is for small groups, the teacher is able to keep in mind specific intended outcomes, and she can adapt her approach and the intended outcome to suit individual needs of the children. 'Match' of work to different children is easy. Calderhead (1984) notes a study of mathematics and language work in primary schools by Bennett and Desforges (1984) where they estimated that just over half of all classroom tasks were inappropriately matched to the abilities of the children. With focused teaching, this inappropriateness would be apparent, and the teacher would easily be able to vary the intended input.

It may be that the reader is at this point thinking that such planning and organization is fine, but limiting in spontaneity. This is nonsense. Detailed planning allows the teacher to make a reasoned judgement on whether or not a new idea *or* the planned activity is more valuable for the child. A total reliance on spontaneity, allowing the interests of the child to take total control, gives the teacher no chance to exercise her professional judgement.

Detailed planning such as I have outlined gives the teacher much greater flexibility than does, for instance, the weekly television programme that often bears no relationship to the other work in the class, or, perhaps equally restrictively, totally guides the work.

Such constraints on the curriculum seem to be totally inflexible as teachers, even when they have access to a video recorder, are loath to miss programme for fear of spoiling continuity, thus emphasizing their reliance on the programme as the basis of their work. I wonder how many teachers who at present rely on 'How we used to live' or 'Zig-zag' are loud in their condemnation of the 'national curriculum'?

The planning system that I have suggested is less restrictive too than reliance on published schemes not closely related to the needs of *your* children. When *you* plan your work, then *you* control its content.

Calderhead (1984) says that:

> teachers themselves must become aware of the nature and effects of their planning and be alerted to the possibilities of their plans being rigid and inflexible and consequently leading to an insensitivity to the teaching–learning process. Plans for teaching, it would seem, might more appropriately act like maps, keeping teachers informed of the route but

always leaving the option of occasional and necessary detours open. Flexibility may have to be planned.

Most teachers plan a broad long-term outline of their proposed 'route', taking into account the majority of controlling factors. However, as the development needs of children cannot be adequately forecast, more frequent planning is needed to interpret these outline plans.

In determining what sort of planning is most effective within the classroom, I favour a rational curriculum planning framework which breaks down into a number of sequential decisions, linked to focused teaching wherever appropriate. The rational framework for planning that I have found to be most useful is that provided by Taba (1962), and is as follows:

   i   Diagnosis of needs
   ii Formulation of objectives
   iii Selection of content
   iv Organization of content
   v   Selection of learning experiences
   vi Organization of learning experiences
   vii Determination of what to evaluate and of the ways and means of doing it.

Within the planning framework that I will now present, the schedule presented by Taba will need to be applied slightly differently at each stage. The decisions made at the early stages will, however, provide a background for decisions that need to be made later.

A suggested system

Diagnozing needs and formulating objectives – the general school framework

We discussed earlier in this chapter the HMI finding that 'knowledge, skills, concepts and attitudes are seen as four key elements of learning to be acquired' (DES, 1987). Many of us would perhaps agree that for a long time we have put too much emphasis on knowledge at the expense of other aspects of learning. There are undoubtedly elements of knowledge that we would expect children to have acquired before they leave the primary school, but if we take the trouble to examine them, they are fairly limited in number.

Most of the skills, concepts and attitudes that we plan for will be best taught and acquired through the medium of topic work, and during the experience a considerable amount of knowledge will be acquired. I would, however, argue that the factual knowledge itself is usually of secondary importance.

Primary schools have always been good at teaching skills,

although when these have not been planned for they are not acquired automatically. It is the belief of some teachers that if materials are offered to children, no teaching is required, as they will simply learn from their experience. Although it can be proved that this does happen, it is a slow process unless the environment and the materials that are made available are carefully controlled. This of course takes careful planning. Skills need to be *taught*.

We have not, traditionally, been very good at systematically planning for concept and attitude development, although we have usually set up environments in which we hope that these developments will flourish.

It is therefore necessary for us to identify the specific knowledge, skills, concepts and attitudes we are hoping to develop. These will depend upon the group of children with whom we are working, and upon their previous experiences. The list will, of course, be drawn up within the framework of the general aims of the school, and will relate to the whole breadth of the curriculum. This list will form the basic objectives or direction of the teaching for the coming year. It will need to be adjusted from year to year to take into account the experiences of previous years, any changes in the composition of the group of children, and any changes in the circumstances of the school.

Ideally, such a list will be drawn up for the whole school, and each teacher will then adapt it for her own use. There is, however, no reason why one teacher, or several teachers within a school, could not draw up their own list of objectives without the involvement of colleagues. Collaboration is however desirable.

In DES (1987), HMI state that 'In Primary schools an activity is rarely limited to one aspect of learning . . . In each case one aspect of the curriculum is the predominant interest, but the work contributes to several areas of learning'. Most primary teachers would recognize this kind of organization. The remainder of this chapter will therefore devote itself to the planning of a 'centre of interest' approach. However, even with this cross-curricular work in mind, to ensure balance over the year it is appropriate at this initial planning stage to identify objectives for all areas of the curriculum. How they are interpreted within the classroom organization is for the teacher to decide.

I have found it useful to draw up a matrix, using the four elements of knowledge, skills, concepts and attitudes along one axis, and the major curriculum areas along the other. Figure 10.1 illustrates this.

The list, if drawn up for the whole school, and by the whole staff, will provide a framework for individual matrices to be taken from it by individual teachers. These matrices will then provide the basic framework on which to build the plans for the year.

Figure 10.1 — Objectives matrix

	Knowledge	Skills	Concepts	Attitudes
Language				
Mathematics				
RE				
History and social studies				
Geography				

Content – long-term planning

Most teachers find that it is important to identify, broadly, an overall framework for the year, listing what topics are to be covered, and roughly when. Identifying ahead in this way ensures that the year fits together as a cohesive whole, rather than a number of topics that are completely unrelated to each other, perhaps suggested by a number of disparate television programmes.

It is at this point that the matrix of knowledge, skills, concepts and attitudes first becomes a useful tool, as it may well suggest topics that would otherwise not be forthcoming. It also serves as a gauge by which to measure ideas that you may already have. Does the topic lend itself to achieving the defined objectives? Is following a topic on Red Indians, based on a television programme, necessarily the *best* way of achieving them?

As mentioned earlier in this chapter, the knowledge that is required to be taught at primary level is minimal in comparison with the skills, concepts and attitudes, and most of the latter three elements of learning can be taught through almost any topic. At this point therefore, the matrix only serves as a guide to choosing topics. It need not be referred to in any detail at this stage.

Still at the long-term stage, but with the topic now decided, the planning begins to become more specific, with the drawing up of the termly or half-termly programme. At these points, with the benefit of evaluation of previous work, web-planning is a very useful tool.

Most teachers are familiar with this technique, and many use webs to plan their work. However, very few develop them to any degree. In generating a 'web' you should *always* try to work with *at least* one colleague (the more the better), even if they are not ultimately going to share in the work.

Taking a *large* sheet of paper, *at least* A2 size, one person writes the topic title at the centre, and everyone then begins to 'brain-dump' ideas. Begin with any idea and work outwards, moving along as many different branches as necessary until no linked ideas can be generated. When that 'pathway' can generate no further ideas, go back to the centre and begin again with a fresh idea. You will find that some 'pathways' will continue to generate numerous ideas; others will fizzle out after a few thoughts. *Do not reject any ideas at this stage* – put down every one that is generated, and do not at this stage try to think about details – the basic ideas are all that are needed. Continue this process for as long as new thoughts come – half an hour will not be untypical. At the end of that time, you should have a piece of paper that will be covered with several hundred ideas. At this point it is appropriate to have a short break before attempting the next stage.

When you return to the 'web', use your list of areas of the curriculum on your matrix (not your objectives) and try to identify whether you have covered each of them sufficiently. If not, this part of the process may well generate a few more ideas, but if it doesn't, don't worry; don't try to force in a curriculum area if it really doesn't fit.

Finally, at this stage, try to see where ideas on different 'pathways' link together, and draw lines between them to show the links.

Figure 10.2 shows the *beginnings* of a web.

If you are sharing the web with colleagues, it should now be placed in a central position, as it will be needed for future stages. With older primary children it is possible to display it for them in the classroom, as some of the ideas may encourage them to investigate areas of the work independently. It is, of course, possible to generate the web with the children.

The next stage is to look at each of the pathways to see which ones interest you, seem the most stimulating to the children, and are the most 'productive' for you to pursue relative to the matrix of objectives. You will have generated many more ideas than you can possibly use. Bearing balance in mind, you should at this point select several that seem the most useful to you for the basis of your work. Do not at this time select too many to work on; you can always return to your web for more ideas at a later stage in the planning process if necessary.

If several teachers are cooperating on the same centre of interest, it is, of course, possible for them each to choose separate pathways to explore with their classes.

Now re-write the pathways you have selected in linear form, at this stage adapting the ideas and disregarding ones that now seem to be inappropriate.

It may be necessary at this stage to re-order the pathways as they are taken from the web – they will have been generated as they came to mind, and may not be in logical sequential order.

It is now time to identify and note which of the activities on the pathways need to be taught, and which areas can be planned as independent work for the children. At this point it is useful to note on the matrix which objectives will be covered in the planned work. Record keeping is dealt with elsewhere in this book, and it is not appropriate for me to mention it in any detail at this point. It is, however, important that every teacher, if possible every school, has a system of not only identifying *what is to be taught*, but also has a way of recording *what learning has taken place*.

As well as identifying what areas of the pathway are to be taught, and what areas are to be worked on independently, it is necessary to plan at this point a number of independent consolidatory activities for each of these.

Each of the 'taught' areas also needs to be classified into one of two groups, those that are best taught as a whole class, and those that require focused teaching within small groups. Those in the latter group need to be classified according to whether mixed or similar ability groups are appropriate.

Figure 10.2 — Topic web

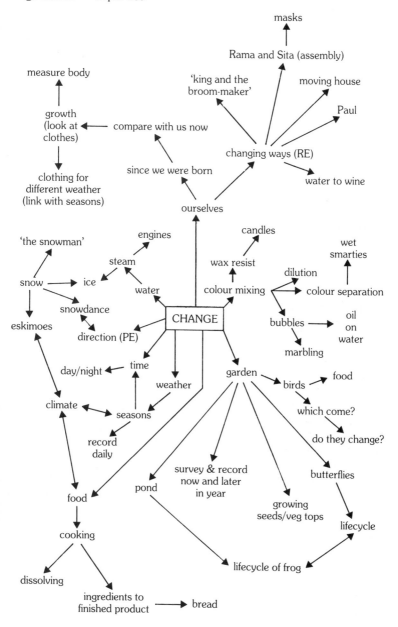

A final topic plan will list the main pathway of taught areas and independent work, consolidation and planned independent development work arising from these, and will allow space for unplanned independent work generated by the children from the work in progress (figure 10.3).

Using this method of planning it is relatively easy to anticipate when a particular part of the activity will take place, and therefore it is at this stage that resources can be booked to be available at the appropriate time.

Although it is being assumed in this chapter that a centre-of-interest approach is being undertaken, it is sensible to assume that there may well be some work that cannot be incorporated into this plan and will run alongside (certain school schemes, for instance). There is nothing that has been said so far that would prevent this taking place. Other work running alongside should be planned as far as possible in a similar way.

Organization of learning – short-term planning

The final part of the planning process is the short-term plan, which is produced weekly, and adjusted daily. This will detail actual times when specific children, as a whole class, in groups or individually, will work on particular aspects of the planned work. It will also identify *what the teacher is doing* at those times.

Two basic types of timetable matrix are possible, one showing the whole week on one sheet, the other showing only one day to a page. A suggested weekly timetable matrix is reproduced in figure 10.4.

An A4 sheet is suitable for such a plan, and a number of copies can be duplicated for a whole term at a time. Each day should be divided up into blocks of uninterrupted time. It is useful to write in unalterable times, such as assemblies and hall PE times, before it is duplicated. Beginning with Monday morning and referring to the long-term plan, the activity planned to take place during the first space on the timetable should be *pencilled* in. If it is planned that group or individual work will be taking place at that time, the *first* activity that is planned should be the focused work of the teacher. This will then remind her that all other work planned for that session should, as far as possible, be independent, and require little of her time. The group of children should be identified by using a code (a group number, perhaps, or a colour), and the activities listed. You will find that if your writing remains fairly small, there is room for up to about six separate groups to be listed in any one session in this way.

Planning of the week proceeds in this way, with constant reference back to the long-term plan and making sure that all children have a

Figure 10.3 — Final topic plan

Main pathway sequence

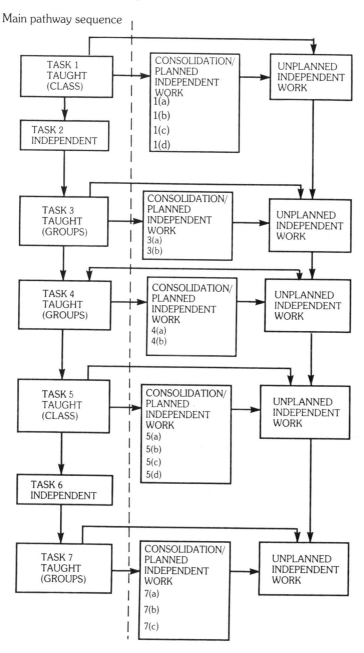

Figure 10.4 — Weekly timetable

	9.00		10.30	10.45	12.00	1.15	5.30
MON	A			PE			
TUE		A				GAMES	
WED		A					MUSIC
THURS		A					
FRI		A		PE			

balanced portion of the teacher's focused teaching. Whenever a group is identified for a focused session, this should be indicated in some way on the plan, so that it is readily obvious to the teacher who she should be spending her time with at any one time.

On a separate sheet of paper, working notes can be made to remind the teacher of the desired learning outcomes, as well as organizational notes. Using this method *all* the children are engaged in productive, planned activities, and the teacher is using her skills effectively, to teach rather than just to oversee activities taking place.

It may well be that for a number of reasons, the day will not go completely according to plan. An unforeseen event may take place, or an activity may lead the class off on a more productive route than was planned. An activity may take longer or less time than was planned.

At the end of the day the teacher must ink in the pencilled plan, altering it where necessary, and this will then be filed at the end of the week as a record of work undertaken. If the day did not proceed as planned, then this may have implications for the rest of the week. One final task is to alter the necessary pencilled tasks for the rest of the week. The plans on the separate sheet will not change, just the timescale on the timetable.

Figure 10.5 — Daily timetable

MONDAY	GROUP A	GROUP B	GROUP C	GROUP D
9.00	←	A S S E M B L Y		→
10.30				
10.45	←	P E		→
12.00				
1.15				
3.30				

If daily planning sheets are preferred, then a timetable matrix similar to that reproduced in figure 10.5 is useful.

Again, an A4 sheet should be used. It should be divided up as indicated, listing unalterable times, and be reproduced with enough copies for the whole term. Planning is then carried out weekly, in advance, but using one sheet for each day. The advantage of a page to a day is that the organizational notes for each group can be written straight on to the sheet. There will, however, still not be enough room for effective outcomes-based teaching notes which will still need to be listed separately.

Whichever system is used, all notes made during the planning process should be filed for reference and as a record both of your thinking process and of the objectives to be achieved.

Conclusion

At all stages in the planning process consideration should be given to evaluating whether objectives are being met effectively, and planning procedures must constantly be reassessed to see if they are helping you as a teacher to achieve them.

Planning is not an end in itself, it is a systematic way to achieve objectives. An old Chinese proverb says, 'If you don't know where you're going, you may end up somewhere else' – planning is essential if purposeful teaching is to take place.

To summarize, I have suggested that you should:

1. Identify the major areas of knowledge, skills, concepts and attitudes to be acquired by the child during the primary stage of education.
2. Identify the major areas of knowledge, skills, concepts and attitudes to be acquired by the child during a particular year.
3. Identify relevant 'centres of interest' through which these can be achieved.
4. For each of these in turn decide on the possibilities using brain-dumping and web-planning techniques.
5. Select 'pathways' through the webs and order them, deciding on what activities need to be taught and which can be tackled independently.
6. Decide which taught elements are best tackled as a whole class and which in smaller groups.
7. Produce short-term plans indicating where you as the teacher are spending your time and identifying what activities each child is undertaking at any particular time.
8. Plan all taught activities in terms of expected outcomes.
9. At all stages, review and evaluate.

Finally, it cannot be stressed enough that systematic planning does not reduce the flexibility of the teaching process, instead it allows the teacher to make a judgement as to the value of the new idea, rather than just being carried along with it whatever its value.

References

Bennett S N, Desforges C W 1984 *The Quality of Pupil Learning.* Lawrence Erlbaum

Calderhead J 1984 *Teachers' Classroom Decision Making.* Holt, Rinehart and Winston

DES 1987 *Primary Schools: Some Aspects of Good Practice.* HMSO

Haigh G 1987 Primary tasks *The Times Educational Supplement* 6 June 1987

House of Commons 1986 *Achievement in Primary Schools: Third Report from the Education, Science and Arts Committee.* HMSO

ILEA 1985 *Improving Primary Schools* (The Thomas Report)

ILEA 1986 *The Junior School Project*

McCutcheon G 1980 How do elementary school teachers plan? The nature of planning and influences on it *The Elementary School Journal* **81**

Richardson N 1984 *The Effective Use of Time.* Education for Industrial Society

Taba H 1962 *Curriculum Development: Theory and Practice.* Harcourt, Brace Jovanovich

11 Record keeping in the primary classroom

Eric Spear

Henry Ford said that history was 'bunk'. There are those who would disagree and claim to see the seeds of the future in the past.

It seems to me that the range of teachers' attitudes to record keeping and record reading parallel the range between these two attitudes to history. There are those who pride themselves in knowing nothing about a child at the beginning of the year in order to give him a fresh start, his name unsullied by any reputation which has, metaphorically speaking, hanged the dog before. They never look at his record because that is now history.

On the other hand, there are those who feel that unless they have the most meticulously maintained charts, graphs, check-lists, standardized test results and detailed profiles on a child's history, they may be unable to make a useful start on any area of the curriculum without doing some inestimable damage to the child.

Naturally, most teachers will not see themselves in either of these extreme positions but will locate themselves somewhere on the continuum between the two. Whereabouts you position yourself may very much be decided by practical considerations as much as your subscription to a particular philosophy of record keeping. Like so much else in this world record keeping is a compromise between the ultimately desirable and the immediately practicable.

The major constraint within which all teachers work is that of the availability of time to perform all the tasks which appear necessary to the teaching–learning process, let alone those which are merely desirable. I want to argue in this chapter that classroom records fall into the 'necessary' category because they are an aid to more efficient and appropriate teaching of individual children and to the curriculum continuity and progression between ages and stages in the education system.

The purpose of this chapter is to offer some ground rules for constructing, maintaining and using records of children's work and development in the classroom by the teacher.

Curiously, the literature on primary school record keeping seems fairly sparse and most literature which touches the subject seems to be mainly concerned with assessment and testing. A notable exception is Clift *et al.* (1981).

All schools keep records of children. There is the medical record maintained by the health authority and often held in the school. There is usually a standardized LEA record card or folder which follows a child from year to year and from school to school throughout his school life. This type of record tends to contain annual summaries of a child's attainment in mathematics and English work; it often includes standardized test scores, particularly of reading, and uses grades like A, B, C, D, E or 1, 2, 3, 4, 5 for achievement and work attitudes; and it has room for comment on social, family and medical aspects. It is cumulative over time, giving a general indication of the trends of a child's progress and achievements. In authorities where there is still some form of post-primary selection, it can be used as an additional indicator of academic potential. Some secondary schools which band or stream children on entry often do so on the evidence of the cumulative primary record card. There are many varieties of LEA record, some good, some not so good, but their purpose is different from that of the classroom record. They are, in practice, periodic summaries of judgements made about children which have been derived from teachers' day-to-day classroom records. What they do not usually offer is much specific indication to the teacher about what the child has mastered and what it is appropriate to teach him next. That is the main purpose of the classroom record.

The designer of any record system needs to bear in mind four main questions in deciding the form and content of the record.

1. Who is going to keep and maintain the record?
2. For whom is the record being written?
3. What do I want that person to know?
4. How will that person use this information?

A record may be used to provide information for statistical purposes. For example, LEAs often keep data on performance in standardized mathematics or reading tests to establish authority-wide trends in performance and attainment of the school population. In this case the performance of the individual is less significant than that of large groups. To extract statistically significant information in this way requires large samples, much larger than a classful of children, so the class teacher will rarely be involved in this type of record keeping.

The keeper and maintainer of children's records in school is usually the class teacher under the general direction of the headteacher. The headteacher may contribute to the record and the school secretary will often be able to contribute factual information about social and medical circumstances. The classroom teacher, however, has the largest share and, thus the largest responsibility in this area. Agreement needs to be reached within the school on the type of records necessary and the purpose for which they are being kept.

The record may form the basis of a written or verbal report to parents and, increasingly, parents are demanding, and being given, greater access to it. Parents will be mainly concerned with how their children are performing in relation to other children of the same age, or in the same class, as well as their child's level of attainment. They will seek reassurance that any problem he may have is recognized and understood by the school and that appropriate remedies are being applied. They will often seek guidance about their role in helping him to overcome difficulties. They will sometimes wish to have their views added to the record or wish to challenge a judgement or correct misinformation as well as to offer new information to the school.

Pupils themselves may have a role in recording their own progress and achievements. This can act as a powerful motivator to pupils and, incidentally, relieve the teacher of a lot of time-consuming, routine record keeping.

Mainly, however, most teachers keep records for themselves, to help remind themselves of things they might otherwise forget, and for other professionals who will have future dealings with the child or the class as a whole. The record, then, becomes an aid to planning the progression of the curriculum for individual children and classes or year groups throughout the school.

The classroom record

The advantage which the primary class teacher has over her secondary colleague is that the former maintains a continuous daily relationship with pupils which is both longer, in the sense of spending more time together, and more comprehensive, in that it covers most of the curriculum areas and implies a more demanding pastoral role than is usually the case in secondary schools.

During the course of the school year the primary class teacher accumulates a vast amount of knowledge about each pupil in the class and stores it in her memory where it is quickly and easily accessible for use. The problem is, of course, that this knowledge is only accessible via that teacher and there will be a time when it needs passing on to someone else, either to a supply teacher or, at the end of the year, to the new class teacher.

Perhaps the best basis for deciding on the form and content of a record system is to place yourself in the position of the receiving teacher and ask yourself what you would need to know about your new class and every individual in it in order to allow an effective teaching programme to be commenced as soon as possible. You will, of course, also need to keep records for your own reference during the year as an aid to planning. Such an *aide-mémoire* is also indispensable when it comes to summarizing a child's achievements on the annual record card.

In these days of national initiatives in education it may not be long before someone comes up with a standard record system for every primary school. This would be a mistake. Clift *et al.* (1981) recommended: 'The formulation of records should always be a collaborative exercise involving all the teachers within a primary school.'

The Schools Council (1983), after suggesting nine areas for which records might be kept, warns:

> It is tempting to suggest that these findings should be used as the basis of a system of record-keeping which would fit all primary schools. Whatever gleams such an idea might bring to a bureaucrat's eye, it seems unlikely to help very much in practice.

The point is that, like everything else to do with the curriculum, the more teachers are involved cooperatively in designing an internal school record-keeping system, the more they are likely to use it effectively because they understand it and have a personal investment in its success. It is an old saw that every school is different. Nevertheless it is true. Despite the recently re-floated idea of a national core curriculum, there will still be variety between schools. This variety is not merely determined by the policy of the school; it is to some extent dictated by the skills and interests of the head and staff, by the catchment area and, sometimes, by the school's physical layout and facilities. In some schools the work of the educational welfare officer, social worker and police is understood only at an academic level. In others there is a wealth of activity-based learning going on! In some schools the population is descended from the last two or three generations in the area, all white, all native English-speakers, nominally C of E. In others there is a diversity of ethnic origin, religion and home language which must have important implications for a curriculum which has previously been taken for granted. If record keeping is a tool for curriculum planning, as argued elsewhere in this book, then the record-keeping system must reflect the individuality of each school's curriculum as well as those aspects which it will, undoubtedly, have in common with all other schools.

The implications are clear. Within broad criteria, schools need to work out their own record-keeping systems, allowing all the contributors and users to participate. Teachers who are going to maintain the records need to be involved, just as those who are going to consult them ought to be able to offer their views. There are some instances where children themselves may be able to contribute to keeping records of their own progress. Many published schemes in language and mathematics, for example, provide for children to chart their own progress and record their own scores on record cards or sheets. In some cases this record can be used in a diagnostic way by the teacher in deciding when a child needs extra help or more practice in a particular area.

Every teacher may have her own private record-keeping system for personal use but that is simply an extension of her own memory. The type of record I want to consider here is the one that other people can consult and understand in the same way as the originator of the record. It is at this level that some agreement is needed between teachers within a school if their records are going to act as a form of communication.

There needs to be agreement on format and content. Commonly understood criteria need to be applied where gradings or assessments are recorded and the derivation of standardized scores needs to be made explicit. If a symbol system is used the record should have an explanatory key. It is not immediately obvious, for example, in a system which uses a scale of 1–5 which end of the scale represents the highest and which the lowest; it needs to be stated.

Content

The Schools Council (1983) suggested in *Primary Practice* nine areas for which records might be kept and it is interesting to compare it with HMI's suggested nine areas of the curriculum:

Primary Practice
1. reading
2. oral language development
3. written language development
4. mathematics (topic)
   mathematics (concepts)
5. social and personal development
6. scientific development
7. study skills development
8. physical development
9. aesthetic development

HMI   (*Primary Practice numbers in brackets*)

1. aesthetic and creative	(9)	6. physical	(8)
2. human and social	(5)	7. scientific	(6)
3. linguistic and literary	(1, 2, 3)	8. spiritual	(5)
4. mathematical	(4)	9. technological	(6)
5. moral	(5)		

I am not sure where no. 7, study skills, fits into the HMI list. It is one of those cross-curricular skills which defies simple description. No overt reference is made in *Primary Practice* to the recording of children's development in moral and spiritual matters though it could be argued that these are covered in no. 5, social and personal development. This is an illustration of the difficulties of trying to define a curriculum both economically and unambiguously. If we are to comment on spiritual and moral development from where do we derive objective values? There are no moral and spiritual tests like those we can apply in some other areas of the curriculum. There is no escaping the responsibility here for making value judgements and such values will need to be worked out with the rest of the staff if some kind of consistency of judgement within the school is to be achieved.

Already the task of recording a child's educational progress begins to look formidable. If it looks formidable for one child it looks downright impossible for thirty or more! The time involved to assess and record each child's progress, rate of development and level of attainment in all of these areas would be a full-time job in itself. 'When,' then asks the beleaguered teacher, 'do I get time actually to teach anything to anyone?'

Part of the answer must be that we cannot record everything in minute detail. If we did we would spend an inordinate amount of time doing it, we would be expecting other people to spend an equally inordinate amount of time in reading and digesting the record and we have to face the strong likelihood that both of these expectations would be unrealistic.

The question of priorities in recording, fairly predictably in the primary school, points in the direction of the three Rs. There are plenty of objective ways of testing a child's reading, comprehension and spelling ability and many aspects of mathematics can be tested in the same way. Indeed, it is in these areas that children can most easily contribute to recording their own scores and charting their own progress.

There are other aspects of these curriculum areas which cannot be judged in such a simple and objective manner, however, and here teacher observation and subjective opinion have to be used. This particularly applies to areas like aesthetic development and study skills development. There are obvious pitfalls here.

If we were going to make the record comprehensive for each child, we would also have to keep detailed individual records on scientific and technological development as well as in history and geography which, I imagine, are subsumed under the social and personal category in *Primary Practice's* list. What about aesthetic and physical development? How much do we record on each individual in these areas?

I think that unless a child shows some relevant and noteworthy interest or ability it is very difficult for classroom teachers to make much useful comment on individual children in these areas. I have doubts whether such areas are susceptible to objective testing in the classroom in a manner which is unambiguous.

In any case, in many classrooms a great deal of this work is done in a cross-curricular manner. That is not to say that these areas are not, or should not be, treated as legitimate areas for separate study in the primary school, just that much topic and project work is bound to see a great deal of overlapping between these and many other areas of the curriculum.

The main record for these areas is going to be a group or class one to show what experiences children have had, how a particular topic has been approached and developed and, perhaps, to comment on any outstanding work by groups or individuals.

The sort of planning instrument teachers often use for topic work is the web, a diagram showing different lines of development which could be pursued from a simple theme. Figure 11.1 gives an example. It would be possible to add the names of children to parts of the web which they had personally developed from their own interest.

This type of class record is especially useful to other, succeeding teachers because it helps to prevent the same topic being tackled again in the same way year after year. It also allows teachers to plan progression to a higher level of skill and understanding where they follow a topic which does overlap with something the children have done previously. Thus, a topic on local history may have had a branch on old photographs which could be the starting point in the future for a topic on photography itself.

The ability to make these connections and develop them is as important for teachers as it is for children and illustrates the unity of knowledge, which is what good primary practice sets out to achieve.

One of the great dangers of record keeping which relies upon a teacher's subjective judgement is that such judgement can be prey to unconscious prejudices. I have sometimes observed that a teacher's comments on a pupil tell me as much about the teacher as they do about the child on whom she is commenting. The danger is not just that teachers may make unjust or unfair comment about a child but that those comments, once committed to a formal record, may be

Figure 11.1 — Topic web

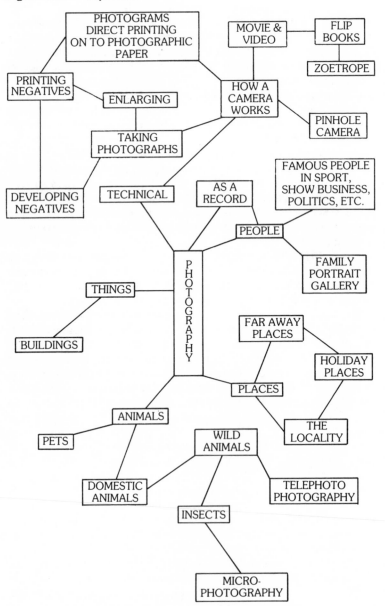

Note: The above can be used both as a plan and a record of aspects of a topic which have been developed with a class.

uncritically accepted by others as definitive, professional judgements.

There is no way of ensuring that this factor is entirely eliminated but it can be minimized. Teachers need, first, to be made aware that they can, unconsciously, allow their judgements about children to be affected by irrelevant factors. Chief amongst these dangers is that of categorizing children as, for example, being less able because they come from deprived homes and then giving priority to observations of those children which tend to confirm this view and ignoring evidence to the contrary. (For a fuller account of this argument see Downey and Kelly, 1975.)

One possible aid to avoiding this pitfall is to come to some agreement as a staff on criteria for making subjective judgements. This will involve, for example, formulating a marking policy, especially for such areas as creative writing where judgements about creative expression can be clouded by poor handwriting, bad spelling or some other factor not directly related to the actual use of language.

Check-lists of these criteria can be a useful way of gaining an overall impression of a child, but they need to be used and interpreted with care for they can lend a spurious pseudo-scientific respectability to what are, after all, subjective impressions. Likewise graphs and histograms which represent judgements rather than objective scores have to be viewed with caution. It is, perhaps, for this reason that the group of teachers I referred to in the opening paragraphs of this chapter prefer to arrive at their own first impressions before reading someone else's last impressions of a child. There is a possible argument here for a two-part record which separates the objective and subjective elements so that they can be referred to separately.

Displaying information

Not only does a record, ideally, need to be easy to maintain, it needs to be easy to read and interpret. The reader of the record will need to have important categories of information clearly distinguishable for speedy reference. The necessity for this is all the greater in situations where the records of a whole class or year group are being compared. It is all very well searching through an interesting and discursive essay on an individual to find out about, say, his ability in reading; it is quite another matter to have to do it for up to 100 children.

The following criteria for the design of a record were made in Clift *et al.* (1981):

1. a clear layout
2. clear, stable printing which will not fade
3. clear section headings
4. the pupil's name in a prominent position
5. sufficient space for comments
6. a prominently placed key (or a user's handbook) to explain the use of abbreviations, symbols and criteria for the assessment of pupils.

Your decision as to the precise format of your record-keeping system will, to a large extent, be dictated by your view of the way a primary school curriculum should be constructed.

If you are wedded to the idea that the curriculum is a hierarchy of pre-specified and very specific objectives then your record keeping will be relatively simple. Just make a list of all the objectives to be attained, starting with the simplest at the top and the hardest at the bottom and tick them off as each is achieved. Thus, the longer the column of ticks, the greater the progress of the pupil (and, some might suggest, the more efficient the teacher).

This is not a chapter on the relative merits of objectives-led and process-led curriculum planning, but if you can't see the drawbacks in the recording system just described then you really ought to read around the pros and cons of objectives in curriculum planning before constructing a record system. (See Kelly, 1977, for arguments in favour of a process model of curriculum planning and Popham, 1963, and Mager, 1962, for arguments in favour of a strictly objectives approach. There are many more!).

If you adopt a process model of curriculum planning then your record system will have to reflect that. The record will be very flexible and open-ended and will contain a description of what happened rather than a description of what merely coincided with the original master-plan which leaves out mention of anything which did not.

Most teachers probably borrow a little from each model in their curriculum planning. In mathematics it is easier to pre-specify objectives than in, say, language because mathematics is more clearly a hierarchical subject where understanding of one concept clearly precedes the ability to understand another. It would be very difficult to sustain a similar claim in the teaching of poetry, drama or art. Of course, there are different levels of understanding in these areas of experience, but 'levels' are very blurred at the edges and overlap to such a degree that a clear, linear hierarchy is difficult to establish.

A mathematics scheme like Nuffield Maths (Longman, 1979) or Kent Mathematics Project (Ward Lock, 1979) has its own built-in recording scheme. This applies to a number of reading and language schemes now on the market. (See Figures 11.2 and 11.3).

Broadly speaking, these records only show what work has been

Figure 11.2 — Nuffield maths record sheet

Nuffield Maths 5-11   Name_____

General editor: Eric A Albany   Date of birth _____

Stage 2 Record Sheet

2

Number

N7	1	Finding the difference.			
N7	2	Counting back.			
N7	3	Taking away.			
N7	4	Recording subtraction.			
N7	5	Practice sheets.			
NS	1	Early grouping activities and games.			
N8	2	Grouping using cubes, etc.			
N8	3	Grouping in tens.			
N9	1	Number bonds up to 20.			
N9	2	Counting on.			
N9	3	Ways of recording.			
N10	1	Difference by matching and counting.			
N10	2	Subtract on by counting back.			
N10	3	Taking away.			
N10	4	Ways of recording.			
N11	1	Recognizing and counting equivalent sets.			
N11	2	Multiplication as repeated addition.			
N11	3	Arrays and the commutative law.			
N11	4	Activities and games for 'table facts' up to 30.			
N12	1	The sharing aspect of division.			
N12	2	The repeated subtraction aspect of division.			
N12	3	Division as the inverse of multiplication.			
N12	4	Remainders.			

Quantities and Shape

S2	1	Sorting for shape and size.			
S2	2	Fitting shapes together.			
M2	1	Reinforcement of coins up to 10p and introduction of 50p.			
M2	2	Breakdown of coins — equivalent value.			
T2	1	Ways of measuring time.			
T2	2	Reading a dial.			
S2	3	Surfaces and faces.			
T2	3	Telling the time (hours, ½'s, ¼'s).			
S2	4	Covering surfaces — leading to area.			
M2	3	Making amounts up to 20p.			
M2	4	Addition — simple shopping bills.			
S2	5	First ideas of symmetry.			
L2	1	Appreciating the need for a standard measure.			
L2	2	Introduction of the metre.			
W2	1	Introduction of kg and ½kg.			
W2	2	Using the kg and ½kg.			
M2	5	Giving change and finding difference.			
M2	6	Subtraction of money (taking away).			
T2	4	Telling the time (5 min intervals).			
C2	1	Introduction of the litre.			
C2	2	Comparing a litre with non-standard measures.			
C2	3	Introduction of ½ litre and ¼ litre.			
L2	3	Comparison with a 10 cm rod.			
W2	3	Introduction of 100 gram weight.			
L2	4	Measuring in cm.			
L2	5	Personal measurement in m and cm.			
T2	5	Simple calculations involving time.			
T2	6	Other units of time.			
C2	4	Cubes, boxes and walls.			

The above record features three rectangles to shade or tick at the end of each concept/activity. This gives several opportunities to record opinions of about a child's experience of and grasp of each category. It can be extended by using the tick/cross system in each recording space (✓ means 'has made a start', X means 'now confident').

Figure 11.3 — Kent Mathematics Project concept network

	3.0	3.2	3.4	3.6	3.8
■ Calculation	Calc. 1 ①	Calc. 2 ②			Calc. 3 ③
● Approx.			Approx. 2 T.1	Approx. 3 T.2 Approx. 4 ④	Approx. 5 ⑤
● Multiplication	Nap. Rods 1 ⑥	Mult. 1 ⑦	Nap. Rods 2 ⑧ Mult. 2 ⑨	Nap. Rods 3 ⑩ T.3 Table Tape 4	Mult. 3 ⑪
● Fractions			Frac. of Circle B.1 Frac. 5 ⑫		
● Decimals & Perc.	Pl. Val. 3 ⑬	Divn. Dec. T.4	Dec. Doms. ⑭	Perc. 3 ⑮	L. Mult. Dec. T.5
● Measurement			*See Level 4*		
● Number Properties	Sq. Nos. ⑯	Series 1 ⑰	Grow. Nos. ⑱	No. Patts. ⑲ T.6	High Score

Matrix Record	Matrix No. _____ No. of Tasks_____		Matrix No. _____ No. of Tasks_____		Matrix No. _____ No. of Tasks_____		Matrix No. _____ No. of Tasks_____	
Level Mean	Raw	Cor	Raw	Cor	Raw	Cor	Raw	Cor
Date Started								
Date Finished								
Matrix %	1	2	1	2	1	2	1	2
Remarks								
Teachers Sig								
	Matrix No. _____ No. of Tasks_____		Matrix No. _____ No. of Tasks_____		Matrix No. _____ No. of Tasks_____		Matrix No. _____ No. of Tasks_____	
Level Mean	Raw	Cor	Raw	Cor	Raw	Cor	Raw	Cor
Date Started								
Date Finished								
Matrix %	1	2	1	2	1	2	1	2
Remarks								
Teacher's Sig								

Note:
The above is a sample of the sheet used to record children's progress through the mathematics programme. Below is the pupils' record which acts as both a forward plan of work and a check on the pace and level of success.

covered. It is necessary to supplement this information with some indication of the degree of success and speed of working of the child. I find a histogram, or bar chart, a very clear way of displaying this sort of information for easy reference. The visual impression is more powerful in communicating the level and rate of progress in areas where measurement in terms of scores is presented. A list of numbers is far less easy to interpret at a glance. Figure 11.4 shows a simple histogram which could be adapted for use in recording scores

Figure 11.4 — Simple histogram record

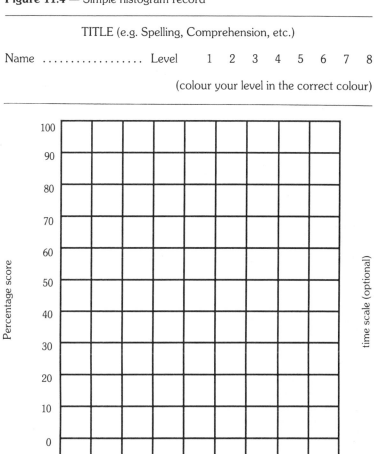

TITLE (e.g. Spelling, Comprehension, etc.)

Name .... Level   1   2   3   4   5   6   7   8

(colour your level in the correct colour)

Percentage score — 100, 90, 80, 70, 60, 50, 40, 30, 20, 10, 0

time scale (optional)

Date ....

Note:
This type of histogram can be adapted for a variety of purposes to record regular scores in mathematics, spelling, comprehension tests and the like. As the child progresses to a different level a different colour can be used to shade in the columns. It would be possible to use two columns at a time, one to record the score and, using a different colour, the adjacent column to record the time taken. The time scale could be indicated on the right-hand vertical axis.

in spelling, comprehension, mental arithmetic, tables tests, etc. Where there are different levels in the scheme these could be indicated by the use of different colours when filling in the chart. Converting scores to percentages will allow for easy comparisons between work done on different occasions and with different scoring levels. The use of a conversion chart or pocket calculator means that even very young children can be trained to do this for themselves. It helps to establish the concept of percentages at a practical level long before it is tackled as a formal mathematical topic.

All such scores, tick charts and histograms need some interpretation, however, and the record must allow space for some teacher comment to provide such interpretation. Teachers' judgements are not infallible, but neither are test scores. The two complement each other. It is useful, periodically, to sum up a pupil's progress and to evaluate it. This evaluation can form part of the more formal part of the classroom record which will be passed on to others for future reference. This will not only thin the file, so that some accumulated material leading up to the summary can be discarded; it will also make for easier reference when someone else needs to consult the record. (Figure 11.5 offers an example of this type of summary record.)

The recording of progress in areas other than the three Rs becomes more problematic because of the amount of time involved and because objective measures of performance are not readily available and are difficult to apply.

The teacher might well keep a book with a page for each child in which she could note particular achievements, interests pursued, extra-curricular activities or any problems, either educational or social, which a child might have. (Figure 11.6 is an example.)

This is moving some way towards the idea of profiling, already taken up at secondary level. It could involve interviewing the pupil about his out-of-school activities and interests. These are often overlooked by teachers but can throw light on unsuspected facets of a child's character and motivation.

ILEA (1985) gives a useful summary of profiling and, though it is obviously aimed at secondary schools, there are some useful pointers for primary practice as well. In particular the idea that a profile should '. . . provide a firm basis for teacher and pupil together to review and plan further learning' is one which will appeal to many primary teachers.

Shipman (1983) has suggested:

> . . . the pupils can keep their own records and evaluate their own work. This ability to self-assess is an important if neglected study skill. Pupils need to be taught to judge their own efforts, and keeping records of their progress is one way to acquiring this ability. This skill can be started early.

Figure 11.5 — Summary record

NAME		DATE OF BIRTH		DATE OF ADMISSION TO CLASS	
STANDARDIZED TEST RESULTS					
DATE	TEST NAME AND TYPE	RESULT	DATE	TEST NAME AND TYPE	RESULT
LANGUAGE					GRADING
MATHEMATICS					
OTHER CURRICULUM AREAS					
PERSONAL & MEDICAL					

GRADING: A = very good, B = good, C = satisfactory, D = below average, E = weak
         (10%)   (15%)   (50%)   (15%)   (20%)

Teacher .... Date ....

Note:
The above summary record is a basic model which can be adapted for personal or school use. It allows the teacher to subdivide the language and mathematics sections and to grade each division separately. Other curriculum areas can be those considered significant at the time of the summary. An indication is given of the meaning of the grades and the average distribution expected.

Figure 11.6 — Class teacher's notebook

NAME	DATE OF BIRTH	DATE OF ADMISSION TO CLASS
CURRICULUM		
EXTRA-CURRICULAR (SCHOOL)		
HOBBIES/ INTERESTS		
PERSONAL & MEDICAL		

Note:
The above is a page from the class teacher's notebook in which she regularly records information which arises randomly as well as recording on a regular and systematic basis subjective observations about the child. If this is done for six children each week then each child will have been the subject of some personal assessment by the teacher about once each half-term. The information gathered in this way will contribute to the summary record (figure 11.5) which will be done perhaps twice a year.

The idea of the pupil commenting on his own work and making a self-assessment is already gaining ground in secondary schools, and I know a primary school where, once a week, pupils discuss their week's work with the teacher and offer an assessment of their own performance. This does not replace teacher assessment, of course, but it does place an onus of responsibility on the pupil. It makes him feel both responsible for judging his own efforts and for setting himself improvement goals. This increase in involvement and responsibility on the part of the pupil can only bring benefit to the whole teaching–learning process in the long run because it will lead to a higher level of self-motivation, which is one of the major aims of education.

Check-list or narrative?

In recent years there have been moves to make the recording of information about children more technical and scientific, and there are schools which have produced elaborate check-lists in mathematics, reading and even in attitude. While there may be attractions for some in this detailed and analytical approach to recording, I have always worried about its real effectiveness. There are, to my mind, major problems associated with such comprehensive and detailed check-lists.

1. They make assumptions about the way teachers actually plan their work which are not valid for most of them. Few primary teachers plan their work in the same detailed, analytical fashion as the check-lists so that the correlation between check-list and work is tenuous and there is a danger that the check-list might operate to distort the teaching programme
2. Keeping such detailed check-lists comprehensively up to date is very time-consuming. My experience, derived from receiving such check-lists from other schools when children have moved, is that such lists are frequently completed in one or two retrospective frenzies during the school year. If they are liable to be used in this way I question the point of such lists. It is obvious that they have not been used as a planning tool to support more effective and appropriate teaching. If it had there would be far more frequent entries. If it becomes an exercise in serving the system, record keeping for record keeping's sake, then I submit there is little virtue in that. Unless records serve the purpose of establishing where a child is and where he should next go in the curriculum the time spent in completing them or referring to them is time not well spent. As Shipman (1983) said, 'Highest priority should be to any activity that produces high benefits in learning for the lowest input of time and energy'. This does not mean that check-lists are entirely without value, just that, as records, they are often not cost-effective in terms of time and effort spent.

3. Unless there is some common understanding between all who write check-lists and all who read them, there is also the problem of interpretation. Does Miss A mean the same as Mr B when she ticks that John knows his seven times table? Are there common criteria being applied? Will a teacher who has never met the compiler of the record have the same understanding of the categories as the teacher who wrote it?

The check-list needs further elaboration and interpretive summary to make it a useful record. As an analysis of the learning stages a check-list can be useful. It can enable a teacher to order and clarify her thinking so that her observations of children's work can be systematic rather than random. The check-list may be a useful aid to structuring her general approach to a particular individual or group, and it will alert her to areas which might otherwise become neglected. As a personal *aide-mémoire* it can be useful, but as a record to be passed on to someone else its value is circumscribed by the shortcomings I have described.

The other extreme of record keeping is to write a detailed, narrative account of the child. Here the teacher, perhaps with one eye on a check-list or other instrument of guidance, can comment at length on curriculum areas relevant to that child and make explicit the basis of her judgements. Because there is little externally imposed structure, the form of the record can be adjusted to suit the features of the child being commented on. There is no imperative to comment on categories chosen by someone else and for which the teacher has no strong opinion. The danger here is that where categories have been pre-specified for the teacher she will be obliged to offer judgements whether she feels she has something relevant to say about that particular aspect of the child or not. The result is often bland and meaningless and, in the case of check-lists, there is frequent recourse to the middle or average column. In a narrative if you have nothing to say about a particular aspect of a child's personality or progress you don't need to say anything.

I have heard teachers say that they find a narrative record very useful because it contains judgements and observations about a child's personality which are derived from lengthy interaction between the reporting teacher and child. There is no short cut to discovering this sort of information for yourself similar to the quick mathematics test or reading test which will yield quick, basic information about a child. Of course all teachers will be alert to the dangers inherent in such subjective judgements about a child and regard them as provisional, but forewarned is forearmed!

The main problem with a narrative record, from the point of view of those consulting it, is that it is time-consuming to extract information from it and, if read quickly, it can lead to important information being missed.

Plainly a record needs to share the most useful characteristics of all the different styles if it is to be useful to a child's current and future teachers. Classroom records need to be in two stages:

1. An extension of the classroom teacher's memory to supplement his short-term planning and to record the level and pace of each child's progress.
2. Periodic summaries using commonly understood and agreed criteria, which will be comprehensible to other teachers, and which will allow smooth transition and continuity of learning at an appropriate level when the child changes teachers.

The format needs to allow for objective test results, teachers' comments and gradings and, where particular mathematics or language schemes are being used, for example, some indication of the level attained, or some reference to the separate and more detailed record which can be consulted for that area. Above all, the information should be laid out in a form which allows quick reference to be made to the particular sorts of information it contains. It should contain reference to the availability of separate, supplementary information and where it is kept. This may be particularly important where a child has a medical condition which may have consequences for his activities both within and outside the classroom.

Finally, there are two simple aspects of record keeping which can be a very valuable way of passing on information about a child. One is the case conference approach where all involved can get together to discuss a child from different viewpoints. Unless there are particular circumstances these case conferences will be between the two teachers involved in the transfer of the child from one class to another. In some situations the case conference may include the head, remedial teacher, educational psychologist, remedial worker or parent. In this situation the pooling of information and the interactive format allow for a clearer and more complete picture to emerge than does a written record alone. The information gleaned from such a conference must itself be recorded and this is best done as a narrative summary with an indication on the main record that this summary exists. This method is time-consuming and only experience will determine for your school how extensively the case conference approach can be applied, bearing in mind the need to observe cost-effectiveness in terms of time.

Particularly valuable to a new teacher can be actual samples of the child's own work. These, included as part of the record, can be a valuable source of information to a receiving teacher because the work can be assessed directly on its own merits and is not subject to the moderating opinion of a third party. There is still a problem of interpretation though, unless it is made clear whether this is a random selection, a typical example (which implies some prior value judgement has been applied) or a piece of 'best' work.

Summary

In this chapter I have offered a consideration of the purpose and uses of record keeping, comments on some of the different formats in common use and have made some recommendations for designing classroom and school record-keeping systems.

I have distinguished between the personal, *aide-mémoire* type of record keeping of the classroom teacher and those more formal records which are handed on for others to use.

I have argued that records are only justified if they are going to be used to plan teaching and learning more effectively. Records which are kept just for the record merely consume valuable teaching and planning time.

I have suggested that records need to be clear and easy to refer to. Important information needs to be summarized and prominently displayed for quick reference.

A record which no one bothers to refer to has little value. This argues for the design of a record-keeping system to be a collaborative exercise between all users to ensure that criteria are commonly understood and applied. Above all this approach will help to ensure that, because of their investment in and commitment to it, teachers will actually use the record system more effectively.

In record keeping, as in all educational endeavour, the acid test is always whether the time and effort spent is justified by the benefit gained. Time and effort are finite and, in the case of time, in short supply, though effort by heads and staff often disguise this fact. In short, unless your record keeping helps to make teaching in your school more effective, discard it and start developing one that does!

References

Clift R, Weiner G, Wilson E 1981 *Record Keeping in the Primary School*. Macmillan

Downey M E, Kelly A V 1975 *Theory and Practice of Education*. Harper and Row

ILEA 1985 *Profiling in ILEA Secondary Schools*

Kelly A V 1977 *The Curriculum: Theory and Practice*. Harper and Row

Kent County Council 1979 *Kent Mathematics Project*. Ward Lock

Mager R G 1962 *Preparing Instructional Objectives*. Fearon

Nuffield Maths 5–11. Longman

Popham W J *et al.* 1969 *Instructional Objectives* (American Educational Research Association Monograph Series on Curriculum Evaluation No. 3). Rand McNally

Schools Council 1983 *Primary Practice* (Working Paper No. 75). Methuen

Shipman M 1983 *Assessment in Primary and Middle Schools*. Croom Helm

12 Classroom review and evaluation

Sybil Coward

The purposes of a review

In order to undertake any kind of review and evaluation it is necessary to be clear about the purposes of it, what benefits there will be from an extra time commitment, and what the implications of the findings might be. The effects of a review and evaluation will be both personal and general, affecting details of organisation and larger aspects of organisation and management.

School buildings vary considerably in size, age, architecture, space available and so on. The variables of necessity make each review and evaluation particular to any one institution. It is because of this and because of the community served that each school and each class teacher not only must understand the positive aspects of a review, but also understand that there are many ways into a review. Gathering information from national sources, LEAs and more local initiatives will provide teachers with an informed base from which to shape their own reviews. Teachers require exposure to the possible before they can focus satisfactorily on the particular. It is helpful for all those considering a review and evaluation of any class space to find opportunities to examine other evaluation models and, through discussion and sifting, to arrive at appropriate starting points for themselves.

A planned review and evaluation should show clearly who the evaluator is, what is being reviewed and why, how the evaluation will benefit the subject of the review and who is the audience for the final report.

The spate of information from DES and HMI along with numerous LEA documents make fulsome statements about the purposes and benefits of review and evaluation. Not uncommonly, they may be found under the heading of 'assessments'. The main purposes are to:

- inform pupils about the progress they are making;
- detect and diagnose learning difficulties experienced by individual pupils;
- contribute information which is relevant to a component of the curriculum;
- evaluate the effectiveness of teaching;
- provide information which will help to improve pupils' learning;
- provide parents and other adults with useful and reliable records of the achievements of pupils;
- assist in the process of maintaining the appropriateness and effectiveness of a curriculum;
- determine the level of development of skills and the acquisition of knowledge;
- provide insights into conceptual development;
- inform on areas of stereotyping;
- know the children better as individuals;
- assist in the development of good teaching and learning models.

A well-constructed review should be regarded as an essential and integral part of the curriculum whose careful preparation leads to further activities resulting from the information gained. A review and evaluation is inseparable from the whole teaching process and focuses the teacher's need to analyse the class space environment, the school ethos and curriculum, and that part of the daily curriculum undertaken within the class.

A review might be of part of the school, of the formal curriculum or of forms of organisation within the school but there has to be recognition that a review of any part of the school cannot be undertaken in isolation and regard must be given to the whole.

Formulating the review of the class space

Where schools have good procedures for review and evaluation of children's needs, abilities, attainments and supporting resources they will be more successful in providing appropriate experiences and work for their pupils than those schools which have not devised such procedures.

Throughout this chapter the term 'class space' is used to refer to any classroom or area of a school in which children are taught. A formal review of a class space begins with a formulation of questions about the children using the space and their needs; the physical area in which their learning takes place and the way in which the whole environment of the class in relationship to the school is used; and the way the teacher facilitates learning and resources the class space in support of the school's formal curriculum. The weighting given to these questions will depend on the ages and stages of development of the children using the class space. For example, a review of a nursery class will include in particular questions about the nature of the children and their emergent abilities to form relationships, moving from the solitary to cooperative interactions; and about the ability to express and inform verbally and substitute some physical actions by using language. A review focused on an older primary class will raise more detailed questions about specific areas of learning and experience, possibly linked to a clear national or LEA policy statement.

Meeting the needs of children in the class space

Stimulation and exploration

Imagine, as an adult, what it would be like to be 5, 7 or 11 years old and standing at the door or entrance to a class space. For the child first experiencing this it might be a bewildering prospect. What would make the child want to stay in that class all day and every day?

The environment must be one that tempts and stimulates the child's curiosity. The more a child sees and hears, the more he will want to see and hear and he will do this until satiated. Pressure from adults at this point could give rise to fear or withdrawal. A failure to stimulate will generate boredom and apathy. A class space that provides new experiences is one that provides for mental growth of the children. There must be interest in novelty, sustained throughout the child's formative years as a healthy source of motivation for further exploration and learning. A well-prepared class space provides for the optimum level which will foster both the cognitive and affective development of a child at any particular stage of growth.

Where the opportunity is provided for the child to explore, be stimulated and explore further, then the child has embarked on the process of learning how to learn and develops an attitude of joy in the sense of mastery and achievement. Children learn best to think, be creative and solve problems in the same way as they learn to read, and that is by doing. The stimulating class space, when reviewed, must show itself as an environment where children can handle, feel and smell a range of exciting objects through informal or structured concrete activities.

A class space that does not allow for exploratory and stimulating activities or where they are disapproved of provides a different set of messages. A child in that environment will develop an alternative set of attitudes to learning and become passive, frustrated, irritable, morose and, possibly, fearful. There will be no sense of joy or satisfaction, only a desire to be away from school.

A class space should be a treasure box of objects and materials where the children can exercise curiosity, a prerequisite for creativity, developing sensory perceptions and a sensitivity to their world.

Len Marsh (1973) wrote:

> Enough has been written to underline the importance of this provided physical environment in relation to the small-scale and, frequently, found natural object. The giant cow parsley, in its autumn 'deadery', is placed in a broken land drainage pipe, or in a fine example of the potter's craft. It stands for sensitivity, a judgement on the teacher's part, and it contributes to the overall aesthetic quality in the room. Its colour and texture contribute to the sense of a good place, to the feeling of a domestic scale rather than an institution.

Meeting the child's need for stimulation and exploration in a class space might be reviewed through the framework of a number of questions on a list which could be endless but is likely to include:

- What use has the teacher made of local exhibits, museums and natural objects for informative displays and interest tables where the materials invite the children to become involved?
- In which ways does a teacher develop interest raised in the class space by visits from members within community services, artists, craftsmen and writers?
- What is there about the room which offers scope for sensory development?
- How is the class space arranged to make first-hand experience possible?
- What importance does the teacher give to the quality of display and stimulating materials available?
- What is the degree of interplay between objects on display, the relevance to the child's real world and other related resources such as books, pictures, charts and audio-visual forms of communication?
- How satisfactorily is the class space equipped for children to make a variety of verbal, written and visual recordings from an initial stimulus?

Does, then, the class space provide a dynamic environment offering a web of interactions and choices through which children learn with the teacher and with each other? A class space is a workshop where emotions are touched and senses sharpened. It is a place where the primary school child continues to learn the qualities of being human. It is a place for an interplay of feelings; a place where children are encouraged to think creatively, sensitively and logically. A stimulating class space is one where emotions, actions and perceptions can be rearranged as children move through learning experiences towards a clearer view of themselves, of others and of their world.

Responsibility

The four needs for stimulation referred to by Pringle (1975), exploration, responsibility, praise and recognition are pertinent to people of all ages. It is because of this that they must receive prime consideration in any review of a class space. Unless these needs are met in the context of the school the learning experience for a child will be unhappy and will leave him without a sense of security and well-being. If any one of these needs is not met within the class the subsequent behaviour patterns of some of the children will make this quite clear to the teacher. Allowing children responsibility is paramount in their education. Too much at the wrong time or inappropriate presentation is not developmental. Part of a teacher's role is to analyse a child's capacity to cope with a given degree of responsibility which should begin with the youngest of children.

Imagine, as an adult, what it would be like to be without any responsibility whatsoever for the period of a few months. An initial reaction might be one of sheer delight at the freedom from it all. But carefully consider what this really means. Perhaps there would be no need to be responsible for keeping either yourself or anyone else. There would be no need to care for any other member of the family, any friend or colleague. Maintenance of self or property would not matter, neither would public or private behaviour. There would be little sense of worth felt in places or events, if concern for others was minimal. In a short space of time the spirit would either degenerate or battle for reinstatement, for it is through the responsibility we take upon ourselves or that which is sought from and granted by others that we recognise and understand our worth and place in society.

Within the class, children need to be given every opportunity to become sensitive to the needs of others and of themselves. They need to learn the skills of responsibility within a framework of heathily developing attitudes, and know when to use them. The class does provide evidence to children of their own adequacies which is reinforced over the years in school. Children, given responsibility at the right level, are secure and assured. They become increasingly confident as their social and interpersonal skills and attitudes develop. They need good models about them: parents, the class teacher, school staff, other peers, older siblings and other adults in their lives. In this imperfect world, where continuity towards responsibility is not clear, the teacher has a most important role in meeting this need.

In a nonsense story written many years ago, a mother declared that her son should not go into the water until he had learned how to swim. In school there is sometimes the temptation, because of a variety of pressures, to allow responsibility only to those who already prove themselves to be responsible. A child cannot learn unless given the opportunity and, like every other skill, responsibility needs to be practised with good guidance from the teacher. The messages received by children about responsibility as they move through their schooling are conflicting and varied. Within the primary years children are best placed to learn cooperation, independence and tolerance. The sense of responsibility has to come from within the child and he will not develop this well unless the teacher also allows him to make responsible decisions.

The skill of the teacher is in knowing where the boundaries are set and what the expectation level is for all the children, and in the clarity of guidance offered through limits, permitted rules and an expected level of sharing.

Watching a class for a relatively short time will give an observer an indication of how much responsibility is expected of, and allowed to, the children. Questions formulated for a review will be about responsibilities towards the physical aspects in the class space and the social interaction between the class space users. They will all be about care and consideration, about thinking, and about avoiding the situation of seemingly mindless action by unhappy and frustrated children. All children, unless suppressed, demonstrate responsible behaviour when presented with good models. The toddler might attempt to comb mother's hair or to help with the baby. Some children of primary school age sometimes have responsibility for younger siblings thrust on them. While they may accept it willingly, care must be taken in the class not to add to a situation that might be burdensome. Caring for living things is an obvious way in which children learn to be responsible. Pets and plants are often a feature of the primary school.

When reviewing the amount of responsibility to be given to children, among the questions posed in a review might be:

- How do they enter and leave the class space and are their movements about the room to some sensible purpose?
- How willing are they to settle to individual tasks by collecting materials and equipment required without recourse to the teacher?
- How well are shelves, cupboards, drawers and units labelled to enable children to remove and return equipment without fuss?

- Are the children able to work easily with peers in small groups or pairs without dispute or disturbance to others?
- How well does a child take care of personal materials and belongings kept in the class space?
- Has each child an appropriate personal space to keep work in good condition?
- How often does the teacher check for tidiness?
- What space has been allowed for larger pieces of work that cannot be housed in personal spaces?
- According to the stage of development of the children, how is the atmosphere conducive to productive working and learning? How much noise and movement is acceptable?
- How much does the teacher do for the children that they should be doing for themselves?
- How much choice are children allowed in planning and developing aspects of their work?
- How far are children encouraged to draft, appraise and develop their own work and that of peers?
- How does the teacher accommodate the need for preparing for work and clearing up afterwards?
- In which ways does the teacher encourage self-motivation and avoid the 'queue for teacher' problem?
- How much responsibility is given to children to manage their own time for tasks or activities?
- Pieces of work may be long or short. What strategies are employed to encourage children to complete tasks?
- In which ways are children encouraged to take care of shared materials and resources?
- How well are children trained to use equipment and resources properly?
- How much time is given to familiarise them with the uses of equipment and resources?
- Where resources and equipment are shared, how is the class organised to make the best sharing possible?
- In which ways are the children encouraged to develop tolerance to others and a willingness to listen to each other?
- What are the established class routines with which children comply and which they feel relaxed about in the class space?
- How much responsibility is given to children to develop their own displays?
- In which ways are trust and mutual respect developed in the class?
- In which ways does the ethos of the school enable children to understand existing rules and contribute to making new ones, if necessary?
- How well do the children care for the personal property of others?
- How is the furniture and equipment arranged in the class space to allow for a variety of working group sizes and ease of access?

This is not an exhaustive list of questions and any review would, by its nature, be selective. However many questions might be raised about how a teacher meets the responsibility need, they cannot be separated from the quality of the relationships formed between the teacher and the children.

Recognition and praise

Hargreaves (1975) writes, '. . . they approve of teachers whose pleasant disposition creates a warm, relaxed friendly climate of personal relationships within which the learning process can proceed.'

Next to parents the class teacher is the one adult in whose care children spend large amounts of time. The attitude of the teacher towards the children as individuals or as a group provides them with a model of adult behaviour which may be similar or very different from that presented by other adults in their lives. Although children have opportunities to form a variety of adult–child relationships, the teacher is a key figure for them all. Most teachers concede that because of the size of classes it is not possible to know all children as well as they would wish. Half a child's life is away from school and the role of child-at-home is one most teachers cannot know other than through contact with parents and observations made of child and parent. This is insufficient to claim total knowledge of any child. Within the class it is the teacher's responsibility to motivate the children towards learning through presenting a framework of favourable attitudes.

The way a teacher motivates children is not always explicit to a class observer but there are several considerations to take into account when planning a review. A range of high motivators should be looked for and these should be evidently worth while in making a positive contribution to the development of children. High motivation begins first with the level of teacher expectation. Most children are more able than is apparent. Assessments of children's activities through what they say and record may conform to a lower level of expectation. Where sensible and sensitive judgements are made about a child's ability and present attainment, then the teacher will be in a better position to guide, encourage and heighten the child's own awareness of what can be achieved.

A stimulating class space will motivate children by the intrinsic interest of objects in it, and through aesthetically attractive displays. The teacher's own personality and interests are motivators where care has to be taken to maintain a curriculum balance, and through them new worlds are opened to children. The class space is a workshop where children make their personal contributions, gauging their success through the comment and actions expressed by the teacher. An encouraging attitude by way of a smile or a nod of approval, by listening to a child and finding ways for children to listen to each other, offers the security and support for learning and a sound base for social and intellectual growth.

Children have a desire to conform and please, qualities on which the teacher can build to generate further the spirit of cooperation. According to Hargreaves (1975), children appreciate a teacher who is able to keep good control; who is fair and has no favourites; who does not give extreme or immoderate punishments; who explains and helps; whose lessons are interesting and who achieves all this while being friendly, patient, understanding and showing a good sense of humour. It follows that such a teacher takes an interest in pupils as individuals. All of this demands much of one teacher with a class of children, especially because human nature does not always allow a consistency of mood; however, most teachers are adept at presenting themselves to their children as caring, motivating professionals.

A class review will also show the low motivators (factors leading to low motivation). Where these factors can be identified, discussions could determine whether their recognition can be used in any way. Among them are parental pressure, an unhealthy degree of competition engendered by the over-importance given to star charts, teams, sex-stereotyping, teacher favouritism, bribery in the form of sweets, teacher sarcasm and reinforcement of a sense of failure. Teachers and other adults within a class space are sometimes unaware of how sharp the senses of primary school children are and refer to children within their hearing as 'not very bright' or 'a bit slow' and say such things as 'You always manage to find the worst one in the class; he's a delinquent, you know'. Promises, threats, bluff, personal appeal, appealing to tradition and mystification are all measures noted as being employed by some teachers at various times. Often the teacher is unaware of the comment or of the effect it has on a child. The whole area of recognition and praise must be carefully considered in a review; in a self-review, a teacher might use a tape recorder to monitor interactions with the children or invite in an observer for this purpose.

Other adults working in the class can be of great benefit here. Discussions with parent helpers relating to the school's policy for parental involvement can enhance the atmosphere in a class and give the teacher an opportunity to articulate attitudes and the process of learning adopted.

This part of the review is usefully undertaken with the help of a fellow professional, perhaps with the use of a video and, less daunting initially, with the use of a tape recorder by the teacher working within the class. Among the questions a review might raise are:

- When reviewing the children's work, how does the teacher ensure that the time is spent effectively?
- What opportunities are offered to the children to talk about their life out of school?
- How well informed is the teacher about a child?
- How frequently is information checked and updated?
- For what purposes and to what extent are children's achievements recorded?
- What are the teacher/school arrangements for parent–teacher consultations?
- Are they had at the best times of the school year to be of greatest value?
- Are school rules and sanctions taken within the class seen to be fair and consistent?
- In which ways do class rules support the ethos of the school?
- What are the safety measures undertaken by the teacher in the class?
- What is the quality of interaction between the class teacher and other adults in the class who may be students, parents or others?
- How well does the teacher plan for attitude development as well as curriculum help with non-teaching assistants?
- How well does the children's work on display show that their achievements are valued?
- How does the teacher encourage an attitude of trust and respect?
- In which ways does the teacher use motivators?
- In which ways does the teacher use body language as signals to the children?
- How interested is the teacher in the children as people?

For many teachers the questions above may be the most threatening aspect of the review because the answers are largely dependent on their personal qualities. What counts is how we bring up children rather than how we present the formal curriculum. Pringle (1975) referred to a review of fifty studies on the way in which teachers' behaviour affects the achievements of their pupils. Two aspects were consistently found to be of importance. They were teacher warmth and teacher enthusiasm; these elicit a better response from individual children and also create a good climate for whole class involvement which, in turn, reflects the attitudes of children to each other and to the teacher.

The formal curriculum

It is not possible to review how needs are met within the class unless aspects of the formal curriculum are also reviewed. When children enter school they bring with them five years of education in life experiences. The teacher's role is to moderate some of these experiences and develop others in the early years at school, while imposing upon the children the formal curriculum of the school relating to requirements of governors, LEAs and central government. Learning, particularly for primary age children, occurs best when there are strong elements of integration across various areas of the curriculum. *The Curriculum 5–16* (DES, 1985) refers to nine areas of experience and learning to which many schools give attention according to a number of variables including size, geography, social intake and so on. However the formal curriculum of the school is presented, it is in the class that the sum total of staff discussions and professional in-service education and reading will have its effect. Turning words into practice is an art at which some teachers are better than others.

Every class space can be aesthetically enhanced. Where the basic class-base provision is satisfactory this can be easily achieved. Where a provision is less than satisfactory in that there are too many corners, ridges, pipes, high fixed cupboards and windows and the space is crowded, then the task is more difficult. Sensitive ingenuity and support are necessary in such circumstances. Where a class space is without basic facilities such as water, power points and appropriate storage, a teacher has to be imaginative and inventive to create not only an aesthetically pleasing area but a usable work room. Many of the questions raised by a review of this aspect will be of a very practical nature and focus heavily on resources. However well or poorly resourced a school is, in whatever building it is housed, is of little consequence if the teacher is in any doubt about forms of organisation that provide the most satisfactory means of presenting the formal curriculum to the children.

The teacher must have a clear idea of what constitutes the formal curriculum. The school will have guidelines and consultants responsible for given areas of that curriculum. It will have identified ways in which continuity, progression and relevance are ensured. There will be a variety of materials and support resources to help in guiding children through conceptual and skill developments which teachers have agreed or are obliged to use. The class space will be used by children of a given age or stage of development. Rationalising the use of a class space to meet the needs of the children and allow for the fullest involvement in the curriculum takes careful planning. Every single item or object in the class space needs to be examined by the teacher, who should question its value. Is it useful to support the curriculum or does it have its own intrinsic interest? To be effective, class spaces should not be depositories for outmoded books, materials and equipment. Time can be valuably spent clearing and rearranging spaces to meet curriculum needs. Often a change of room prompts such an evaluation, which needs to be continuous.

Some resources, of necessity, will be kept in other parts of the building and will be available for use on a shared basis, but basic resources should be within the class at all times. Unless there is no alternative because of the physical constraints of the building, no piece of equipment should be introduced and no organisational arrangement of furniture and fittings should be undertaken unless the educational purpose is very clear to the teacher. An effective classroom environment is complex. It supports a variety of sizes of groupings for specific reasons, and within it there are work areas resourced for specific experiences. Part of the teacher's preparation is to provide requisite materials for the children to pursue practical knowledge and planned activities.

The questions devised for this part of the review might relate to areas of experience and learning but will also question the quality of understanding and recording.

Aesthetic and creative

- What is the range of aesthetically stimulating collections available to the class?
- What access is there to good quality pictures, natural objects, carvings and models?
- Is the class well resourced with a range of art papers, brushes of various thicknesses, a variety of drawing implements, etc.?
- How effective is the range of tools and equipment? Are scissors able to cut, etc.?
- What scope is there for a range of three-dimensional activities?
- What floor space, large areas and surfaces are available?
- What opportunities are offered for small group exploration of sound?
- What provision is there to enable role play to happen?
- In which ways are malleable and rigid materials stored?
- What scope is there for children to learn the language related to the different aspects of this area of learning and experience?

Many of these questions have an applicability to other areas of the curriculum.

Human and social

- In what ways are children enabled to understand their world through access to information from books, charts, maps, globes, pictures, etc.?
- What first-hand experiences are made available to the children through the immediate environment?
- What attention is given to the pursuit of relevance, accuracy and reality?
- In which ways are children guided towards developing concepts in geography, history and the environment?

- What are the necessary working tools and equipment for tasks related to this area of the curriculum? Are they available and in good order?
- In what ways is the language related to this area used and developed?

Linguistic and literary

- In which ways does the class space accommodate books, book displays, audio-visual equipment, a library area? Do these reflect the linguistic needs of the children?
- How does the teacher encourage the presentation of the children's written work?
- In which ways are the children encouraged to discuss ideas, plan topic work and plan and present displays?
- What opportunities are presented for the children to develop a variety of forms of writing and how well does the timetable allow for drafting, long pieces of work, individual and group work?
- What opportunities have the children for learning and using language specific to each curriculum area?
- How well does discussion and written work support first-hand and practical experiences?
- What scope is there within the class space for drama?

Mathematical

- In which ways are the children encouraged to explore mathematically?
- How well is the class equipped to provide for a full range of concrete activities?
- What scope is there for solving real problems through mathematics?
- In which ways are mathematical concepts and skills used in other areas of the curriculum?

Physical

- How has the furniture in the class been arranged to allow the maximum freedom of movement?
- How have materials and equipment been arranged for best access by the children?
- To what extent does furniture – chairs, tables, etc. – fit the size of the children?
- How well ventilated is the class space?
- Is it a physically comfortable working atmosphere?
- Is there access to the outside nearby?

Moral and spiritual

- How well do the interest collections stimulate and inform the children of the attitudes and beliefs of others?

- How well does the class reflect a balance in the curriculum towards understanding a variety of beliefs?
- How well do the class resources avoid stereotyping and prejudice?

Scientific and technological

- What opportunities are offered to children to discover the properties of materials?
- What opportunities are offered to make observations, comparisons and recordings?
- How well is the class resourced to allow children to explore and experiment?
- In which ways are the children encouraged to estimate and hypothesise?
- What opportunities are offered to children to work with and care for living things?
- What applications are children encouraged to make of their developing understanding of energy and force?

Towards development

Each area of the curriculum will be supported by guidelines to which details for assessing children's attainments may be related. The questions set out here might be addressed by individual teachers or by staff groups. Ensuing discussions might focus on this approach to a class space review and offer both support and a platform for controversy. There may be implications for the aims of the school too, embodying a move toward greater flexibility. *Education 5–9* (DES, 1982) identified satisfactory classes as those where there is a satisfactory balance between the opportunities provided for the children to find out things for themselves and more formal teaching; and where there is a good balance between activities initiated by the teacher and those chosen by the children. Class arrangements need to remain flexible and the environment needs to be aesthetically pleasing and intellectually challenging. It should embody the children's interests, evoking questions and stimulating discussion. It is a place where children can experiment and be creative with a wide variety of materials.

Perhaps the most important role of the teacher is that of opening new worlds to the children in which their human needs are met, a balance is achieved between cognitive and affective learning for the well-motivated class, and teaching methods and processes for learning are geared to maximising the strengths of children and minimising their weaknesses. Any review of a class space must take account of the reviewer's own skills and experiences, how flexible and open the thinking is, how perceptively the questions have been formulated and whether there is any bias. An honest review will enable the participating teachers to gain a greater depth of understanding in their work, and provide them with a good basis for future development.

References

DES 1982 *Education 5-9: an Illustrative Survey of 80 First Schools in England*. HMSO
DES 1985 *The Curriculum 5-16 (Curriculum Matters 2)*. HMSO
Hargreaves D 1975 *Interpersonal Relationships and Education*. RKP
Marsh L 1973 *Being a Teacher*. A & C Black
Pringle M K 1975 *The Needs of Children*. Hutchinson

Further reading

Curtis A M 1986 *A Curriculum for the Pre-school Child*. NFER-Nelson
de Bono E 1976 *Teaching Thinking*. Temple Smith
DES 1978 *Primary Education in England*. HMSO
DES 1984 *English from 5-16 (Curriculum Matters 1)*. HMSO
DES 1985 *Mathematics from 5-16 (Curriculum Matters 3)*. HMSO
DES 1985 *Music from 5-16 (Curriculum Matters 4)*. HMSO
DES 1985 *Home Economics from 5-16 (Curriculum Matters 5)*. HMSO
DES 1985 *Quality in Schools: Evaluation and Appraisal*. HMSO
DES 1985 *Science 5-16: a Statement of Policy*. HMSO
DES 1986 *Health Education from 5-16 (Curriculum Matters 6)*. HMSO
DES 1986 *Geography from 5-16 (Curriculum Matters 7)*. HMSO
Jones T P 1972 *Creative Learning in Perspective*. University of London Press
Schools Council 1983 *Primary Practice*. Methuen

Contributors

Ray Arnold has been headteacher of Redriff Primary School in the Surrey Docks area of Bermondsey, London, since 1979. During the 1987/88 school year he is seconded to the ILEA Primary Management Studies Centre to help with the design and delivery of management courses for teachers.

John Barrett is a Primary Adviser in West Sussex. He was previously the headteacher of two schools, one primary and one junior, in Hampshire.

John Bird is head of Meadow Farm Primary School, Chaddesden, Derby, and has been in the forefront of community education in Derbyshire. He entered teaching late after working in the coal mining industry. During the school year 1984/85 he was seconded to Derbyshire LEA as an Advisory Headteacher.

Sybil Coward is Primary and Early Years Inspector for Kent. She was previously a headteacher in West Sussex, and a Primary Adviser in Hampshire. She has worked extensively throughout the United States.

Ian Craig is Inspector for Primary Education, London Borough of Croydon. He was previously headteacher of two primary schools in Kent. He is Reviews Editor and Associate General Editor of the journals *Educational Management and Administration* and *Management in Education*.

Helen Gillespie is head of Twydall Infant School, Kent, and is an executive member of the Kent branch of the National Association of Headteachers.

Kath Rollisson is a Primary Adviser in Humberside. She has been the headteacher of an infant school in the Dockland area of Salford, and the head of an open-plan primary school in Rochdale.

Iain Smithers is a lecturer/tutor in the Primary Education Department of the Northern College of Education, Aberdeen. He was previously the headteacher of an open-plan primary school.

Eric Spear is head of Staplehurst Primary School in Kent, his second headship in the UK. He has also been a headteacher in Swaziland. In 1984 he was one of the first headteachers to attend an 'OTTO' management course, and since then has himself regularly contributed to management training courses.

Heather Toynbee is headteacher of Hawkedon Primary School, Reading. She was previously a headteacher in Northamptonshire, and has taught in Surrey. She is currently vice-chairperson of the Berkshire branch of NAPE.

Tony Wainwright is Principal Primary Adviser for Dorset. He took up this post in 1986, having been a Primary Phase Adviser for Berkshire for the previous seven years. Prior to this he was the head of one primary, and two middle schools.

Clive Wilkinson is Adviser for Primary Education, Gloucestershire. He has worked as a teacher and headteacher in open-plan schools in Hampshire and Berkshire, and has a national reputation for his work on the teaching of handwriting.

Index